GASOLINE PRICES AND THEIR EFFECTS ON BEHAVIOR

AMERICA IN THE 21ST CENTURY: POLITICAL AND ECONOMIC ISSUES

Public Administration, NGO's and Public Debt: Issues
and Perspectives
Marcel Kratochvil and Valentin Pokorny (Editors)
2010. ISBN: 978-1-60741-597-8

Crossing Cultures - Stories of the Peace Corps Experience
Paul D. Coverdell (Editor)
2010. ISBN: 978-1-60876-091-6

Globalized Supply Chains and U.S. Policy
Solomon Mensah (Editor)
2010. ISBN: 978-1-60876-133-3

Role of Tax Preferences in Financial Infrastructure
Michael D. Scott (Editor)
2010. ISBN: 978-1-61668-546-1

Role of Tax Preferences in Financial Infrastructure
Michael D. Scott (Editor)
2010. ISBN: 978-1-61668-726-7 (E-book)

AMERICA IN THE 21ST CENTURY: POLITICAL AND ECONOMIC ISSUES

GASOLINE PRICES AND THEIR EFFECTS ON BEHAVIOR

HERMANN SCHREIBER
EDITOR

Nova Science Publishers, Inc.

New York

LIBRARY OF CONGRESS CATALOGING-IN-PUBLICATION DATA
Gasoline prices and their effects on behavior / editor, Hermann Schreiber.
    p. cm.
Includes bibliographical references and index.
ISBN 978-1-60741-351-6 (softcover)
1. Gasoline--Prices--United States. 2. Automobiles--Fuel consumption--Standards--United States. 3. Automobile industry and trade--United States. 4. Energy consumption--United States. I. Schreiber, Hermann, 1945-
 TL151.6.G375 2010
 338.4'3665538270973--dc22
                        2009039024

Published by Nova Science Publishers, Inc. † *New York*

CONTENTS

PREFACE

In January 2003 the average retail price for a gallon of gasoline in the United States was $1.50—roughly equal to the real (inflation-adjusted) price during much of the preceding half-century. Since then, the price of gasoline has risen sharply. It was last below $2 per gallon in February 2005, and for much of 2007, prices topped $3 per gallon (see Summary Figure 1).

This Congressional Budget Office (CBO) study examines the scope and intensity of consumers' responses to the upward trend in gasoline prices that began in 2003. Those responses have been large enough to interrupt a pattern of steady growth in total gasoline consumption dating back to 1990, the last time U.S. gasoline prices rose substantially.[1] If current high prices—and consumers' responses to them—persist, the effect on overall gasoline consumption will grow stronger as older, less-fuelefficient vehicles are retired and as consumers consider other, less easily implemented adjustments to their patterns of consumption.

The 100 percent increase in real U.S. gasoline prices since 2003, which is larger even than the record increases of the early 1 980s, has induced motorists to adjust their driving habits and the types of vehicles they purchase. Those responses have important implications for the future fuel efficiency of the passenger vehicle fleet, for the way vehicles are driven, and for the use of the nation's highway and mass transit networks should higher gasoline prices persist. The findings of this study are thus relevant in assessing the impact of policies that seek to encourage greater fuel economy and promote more-efficient patterns of driving.

In preparing this study, CBO analyzed data on trip frequencies and speeds on several California highways from 2003 to 2006. CBO also gathered and analyzed data on U.S. sales of new and used vehicles over the same period.

The data show that consumers have responded in a variety of ways to higher gasoline prices. The effect has thus far been small, which is consistent with current estimates of the short-run responsiveness of gasoline consumption to changes in price. That effect would be expected to increase if prices remained high.[2]

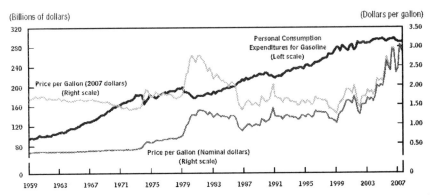

Source: Congressional Budget Office based on data from the Department of Commerce, Bureau of Economic Analysis.

Notes: Consumer expenditures are for gasoline and motor oil through October 2007 (motor oil is about 1.5 percent of the total).

Consumer expenditures were adjusted by CBO using the Bureau of Economic Analysis's (BEA's) chained price index for gasoline and other motor fuel. Changes in expenditures reflect changes in gallons consumed. Real gasoline prices were calculated by CBO using BEA's consumer price index for all urban consumers.

Summary Figure 1. Personal Consumption Expenditures for Gasoline and the Average Price of Gasoline in the United States.

CBO has found the following specific effects in its analysis:

- Freeway motorists have adjusted to higher prices by making fewer trips and by driving more slowly. CBO analyzed data collected at a dozen metropolitan highway locations in California, along with data on gasoline prices in California, to identify changes in driving patterns. On weekdays in the study period, for every 50 cent increase in the price of gasoline, the number of freeway trips declined by about 0.7 percent in areas where rail transit is a nearby substitute for driving; transit ridership on the corresponding rail systems increased by a commensurate amount. Median speeds on uncongested freeways declined by about three-quarters of a mile per hour for every 50 cents the price of gasoline has increased since 2003.

- After increasing steadily for more than 20 years, the market share of light trucks (including sport–utility vehicles and minivans), relative to all new passenger vehicles, began to decline in 2004. As a result, the average fuel economy of new vehicles has increased by more than half a mile per gallon since 2004 (because light trucks tend to be less fuel efficient than cars).

- Used-vehicle prices have shifted, reflecting changing demand, particularly with respect to fuel economy: The average prices for larger, less-fuel-efficient models have declined over the past five years as average prices for the most-fuel-efficient automobiles have risen.

CONSUMERS' RESPONSES TO HIGHER GASOLINE PRICES

Recent research suggests that consumers are not very responsive to changes in the price of gasoline, at least in the short run. (Increased expenditures on gasoline have, however, reduced consumers' saving, real income growth, and probably other forms of consumption.)[3] For a variety of reasons, consumers are currently only about one-fifth as responsive to short-run changes in gasoline prices as they were several decades ago. That decline in sensitivity has been attributed to growth in real income, which has rendered gasoline a smaller share of consumers' purchases from disposable income. Price sensitivity also has declined because a gallon of gasoline takes a car farther than it did in the past, in part because of fuel economy standards. Finally, the development of distant suburbs also has contributed by making some consumers more reliant on the automobile. The longer commutes are balanced by lower housing costs.[4]

The research suggests that a 10 percent increase in the retail price of gasoline would reduce consumption by about 0.6 percent in the short run.[5] Over a longer period, consumers would be much more responsive to an increase in the price of gasoline (should the higher price persist) because they would have more time to make choices that took longer to put in place, such as buying an automobile that gets better gasoline mileage. Estimates of the long-run elasticity of demand for gasoline indicate that a sustained increase of 10 percent in price eventually would reduce gasoline consumption by about 4 percent.[6] That effect is as much as seven times larger than the estimated short-run response, but it would not be fully realized unless prices remained high long enough for the entire stock of passenger vehicles to be replaced by new vehicles purchased under the effect of higher gasoline prices—or about 15 years. Over that time, consumers also might adjust to higher gasoline prices by moving or by changing jobs to reduce their commutes—actions they might take if the savings in transportation costs were sufficiently compelling. Those long-term effects would be in addition to consumption savings from short-run behavioral adjustments attributable to higher fuel prices.

Driving Behavior

Underlying the market's overall response to higher gasoline prices are some specific short-run adjustments in the way people drive. To estimate the importance of those adjustments and how they contribute to the response to higher gasoline prices, CBO analyzed two sets of data: One consisted of detailed information on traffic flows at multiple freeway locations in California; the other contained measurements of vehicle speeds at some of those locations.

California was chosen because its highway system has an extensive network of automatic data collection devices that have recorded large quantities of traffic data from many locations over long periods. (More information about the data and how they were collected is provided in Appendix A.) Although CBO's analysis is based on data from California, the findings should apply to metropolitan areas in other states to the extent that those areas are similar in terms of drivers' ages and income, the vehicle stock, highway configuration, and enforcement of speed limits.

Many of the freeways CBO studied run parallel to light- or heavy-rail transit systems, so it is possible to discern the effects of gasoline prices on daily vehicle flow in the presence or absence of an accessible rail transit alternative to driving. CBO's study also took into account the time of day, day of the week, season, road characteristics, and other factors that influence the way motorists drive.

CBO's analysis indicates that, since 2003, for every nominal increase of 50 cents per gallon in the price of gasoline, median driving speeds on uncongested urban freeways have declined by about three-quarters of a mile per hour, on average, and the amount of weekday traffic on freeways next to commuter rail systems has declined by about seven-tenths of a percent. Those adjacent commuter rail systems also are affected by higher gasoline prices: The increase in the number of passengers per day on those systems is approximately equal to the decline in the number of vehicles on the adjoining freeways. Those effects, although fairly small, are highly consistent with recent estimates of the short-run elasticity of demand for gasoline.

Purchases of New Vehicles

If sustained, higher gasoline prices would increasingly influence consumers' automobile-buying habits. Consumers typically own a vehicle for several years, during which time little can be done to affect that vehicle's fuel economy. Consumers who are considering replacing a vehicle are more likely to buy a more-fuel-efficient vehicle the higher they expect gasoline prices to be during the time they own their next vehicle.

Thus, with rising gasoline prices, in 2004 the market share of light trucks began to decline relative to that of cars. That year, light trucks constituted about 55 percent of the passenger vehicle market; by 2006, that proportion had slipped below 52 percent. The decline occurred despite slight increases in financial incentives to promote the purchase of light trucks in 2006 and a slower average rate of increase in suggested retail prices compared with those for cars.

Consistent with a shift in the mix of vehicles sold, the higher gasoline prices of the past several years have contributed to an increase of more than half a mile per gallon in the combined average fuel economy ratings of new cars and light trucks since 2004. A primary cause has been the decreased market share of light trucks, which average fewer miles per gallon than cars do. But light trucks also have become more fuel efficient, a trend that began in 2003 and that has been spurred on by the adoption of more-stringent fuel economy standards beginning with the 2005 model year. The average fuel economy of new cars also has increased somewhat in nearly every model year since 2000—the first sustained increase since the mid-1980s. (In 2000, average real gasoline prices also reached levels not seen since the mid-1980s.) That such an increase occurred despite slightly larger annual price increases for more-fuel-efficient vehicles (a pattern that carried over to used-vehicle markets) is a further indication of an increase in consumer demand for fuel economy.

The increase in fuel economy among new vehicles over the past few years has partially offset the 1.9 mile per gallon (mpg) decline that occurred from 1

987 through 2004.[7] Should higher gasoline prices persist over the next decade or more, and should consumers continue to respond to those prices as they have done over the past few vehicle model years, the increase in fuel economy eventually will be reflected throughout the fleet rather than, as currently, only in passenger vehicles from the past few model years.

GASOLINE PRICES, POLICY, AND TOTAL GASOLINE CONSUMPTION

The nationwide increase in gasoline prices since 2003 has not merely slowed the rate of growth in gasoline consumption. Through the third quarter of 2007, real consumer purchases of gasoline—which can be thought of as a measure of quantities consumed—had fallen slightly in 8 of the preceding 1 0 quarters, compared with purchases the year before (see Summary Figure 1). Such declines, although small, occurred despite continued population growth, changing patterns of residential development and job location, and technological change, all of which have encouraged the increasing consumption of gasoline, particularly in recent decades.

The increase in gasoline prices and the response of consumers to higher prices have important implications for government policies that would reduce gasoline consumption. Such policies can produce better outcomes for society than would result from pure market forces, because the consumption of gasoline imposes social costs—environmentally damaging emissions, for example—that are not reflected in the price of gasoline.

Two important policy tools that encourage people to drive more-fuel-efficient vehicles (and thus reduce gasoline consumption) are the federal corporate average fuel economy (CAFE) standards and federal and state gasoline taxes.[8] CAFE standards require manufacturers to design and sell larger numbers of fuel-efficient cars and light trucks than the market would otherwise demand. Higher taxes reduce gasoline consumption by raising the retail price of gasoline, with the same effects on driving behaviors and vehicle choices that would result from a market-driven price increase. In contrast, stricter CAFE standards, while reducing gasoline consumption, also reduce the per-mile costs of driving and thus partially offset the effects of higher gasoline prices on total miles driven and on freeway speeds.

Higher prices for gasoline affect both types of policies. By increasing the market demand for fuel-efficient vehicles, higher gasoline prices reduce the economic costs—to manufacturers and to consumers—of achieving stricter CAFE standards. Also, with higher gasoline prices, the average gasoline tax—or any given increase in that tax— is now a smaller share of the price of gasoline than it was in the past. (The average gasoline tax, including state levies, is currently about 46 cents per gallon, of which 18.4 cents is the federal tax.) Consequently, a given (cents per gallon) increase in the gasoline tax would have a smaller effect on fuel economy in new vehicles and on fuel-saving changes in the way motorists drive. However, because the higher gasoline prices would themselves encourage greater fuel efficiency, a smaller tax would be needed if that were the policy goal.

End Notes

[1] Similar episodes also occurred in 1974 and 1979 in conjunction with Mideast oil supply interruptions. The current increase has several origins, including higher prices for crude oil caused by increased global demand, higher-than-usual refinery costs, and larger price markups. See, for example, Federal Trade Commission, *Gasoline Price Changes: The Dynamic of Supply, Demand, and Competition* (2005), www.ftc.gov/reports/gasprices05/ 050705gaspricesrpt.pdf; and *Investigation of Gasoline Price Manipulation and Post-Katrina Gasoline Price Increases* (2006), www.ftc.gov/reports/060518PublicGasolinePricesInvestigation ReportFinal.pdf.

[2] The short-run responsiveness, or *elasticity,* of consumption to changes in price reflects adjustments that consumers can easily (in some cases, spontaneously) make, without any major investment. By contrast, the long-run elasticity is greater because it reflects the effects of additional choices that arise over a period of years, including vehicle purchases and decisions about where to live in relation to one's place of work.

[3] See Congressional Budget Office, *The Economic Effects of Recent Increases in Energy Prices* (July 2006).

[4] For a discussion of increased reliance on the automobile, see Matthew E. Kahn, "The Environmental Impact of Suburbanization," *Journal of Policy Analysis and Management,* vol. 19, no. 4 (2000), pp. 569–586. For information on the decline in fuel costs' share of disposable income, see Jonathan E. Hughes, Christopher R. Knittel, and Daniel Sperling, *Evidence of a Shift in the Short-Run Price Elasticity of Gasoline Demand,* Research Report UCD-ITS-RR-06-16 (University of California, Davis, Institute of Transportation Studies, 2006); and Kenneth A. Small and Kurt Van Dender, "Fuel Efficiency and Motor Vehicle Travel: The Declining Rebound Effect," *Energy Journal,* vol. 28, no. 1 (2007), pp. 25–51. For information on the decline of fuel costs as a share of total driving expenditures, see Ian W.H. Parry and Kenneth A. Small, "Does Britain or the United States Have the Right Gasoline Tax?" *American Economic Review,* vol. 95, no. 4 (2005), pp. 1276–1289; and Hughes, Knittel, and Sperling, *Evidence of a Shift in the Short-Run Price Elasticity of Gasoline Demand.*

[5] See Hughes, Knittel, and Sperling, *Evidence of a Shift in the Short-Run Price Elasticity of Gasoline Demand,* and Small and Van Dender, "Fuel Efficiency and Motor Vehicle Travel." With the relatively small price elasticity, moderate price increases may cause the *growth* in consumption to decline even as total consumption continues to rise, because gasoline consumption depends on factors other than price: Growth in the population and in the number of registered vehicles and drivers, for example, leads to increases in total

consumption. A sizable increase in price would be required to completely neutralize those factors and cause total consumption to decline.

[6] A 1996 federal report proposed a value of -0.38 for long-run price elasticity. See Department of Energy, Office of Policy and International Affairs, *Policies and Measures for Reducing Energy Related Greenhouse Gas Emissions: Lessons from Recent Literature,* DOE/ PO-0047 (July 1996). That value was used by the Congressional Budget Office in *Reducing Gasoline Consumption: Three Policy Options* (November 2002) and in *The Economic Costs of Fuel Economy Standards Versus a Gasoline Tax* (December 2003). Kenneth A. Small and Kurt Van Dender, in "Fuel Efficiency and Motor Vehicle Travel," estimate a similar long-run price elasticity value of -0.43. Higher estimates exist, but they come primarily from the 1970s and 1980s and from international studies. For a survey, see Daniel Graham and Stephen Glaister, "The Demand for Automobile Fuel: A Survey of Elasticities," *Journal of Transport Economics and Policy,* vol. 36 (2002), pp. 1–26.

[7] In some of the intervening years, average fuel economy increased, but never by more than 0.2 mpg. CBO's calculations of average fuel economy are based on annual vehicle sales and closely mirror the Environmental Protection Agency's calculations based on model year sales. (See Environmental Protection Agency, *Fuel Economy,* www.epa.gov/fueleconomy.)

[8] For an analysis of the correspondence between gasoline taxes and CAFE standards, in terms of fuel savings, see Congressional Budget Office, *The Economic Costs of Fuel Economy Standards Versus a Gasoline Tax.* That analysis is based on a gasoline price of $1.50 per gallon, but the same methodology can be used with different gasoline prices. For national average gasoline taxes as of March 2007, see American Petroleum Institute, www.api.org/policy/tax/stateexcise/upload/March_2007_gasoline_and _diesel_summary_pages.pdf.

In: Gasoline Prices and their Effects on Behavior   ISBN: 978-1-60741-351-6
Editor: Hermann Schreiber   © 2010 Nova Science Publishers, Inc.

Chapter 1

GASOLINE PRICES AND DRIVING BEHAVIOR*

Congressional Budget Office

The effects of rising gasoline prices can be seen in changing highway traffic volumes and speeds and in shifting consumers' choices about the kinds of vehicles to drive. In the short run, rising gasoline prices affect the number of vehicles on the highway and the speeds at which those vehicles are driven in free-flow conditions. It is a simple matter for motorists who make such behavioral adjustments to undo them if gasoline prices decline. Other adjustments motorists could make—including changing the kinds of vehicles to buy or where to live or work—are not as easily reversed. The greater price sensitivity of gasoline consumption in the long run reflects those other adjustments.

This Congressional Budget Office (CBO) study illustrates both kinds of effects that rising gasoline prices have had on consumers, and it suggests the kinds of consumer effects that could be expected from policies that would seek to discourage gasoline consumption and, by extension, limit the associated carbon dioxide emissions.

CBO's analysis of the influence of gasoline prices on motorists' behaviors is based on four years of data collected from metropolitan freeways in California between 2003 and 2006 and on statewide average gasoline prices and wages over that period. (Appendix A describes the data used, and

---

* This is an edited, reformatted and augmented version of a Congressional Budget Office publication dated January 2008.

Appendix B explains CBO's analytical approach and presents the econometric results of the analysis.)

VOLUME OF TRAFFIC

One way motorists can reduce transportation costs is to drive less, for example by using public transportation, alternative modes of transportation, or car pools; by consolidating trips; or by telecommuting to work. They also might make shorter trips, substituting nearby recreation or shopping locations for more-distant alternatives that they otherwise prefer or, in the long run, they might move closer to work or choose jobs closer to home.

The likelihood that a driver will make one of those changes depends on the price of gasoline and on other factors that determine how attractive driving is compared with the alternatives. For a motorist who routinely faces heavy traffic or high parking fees, the benefit of switching to public transportation can be quite large. But motorists who previously had been willing to accept those costs without switching must therefore place a relatively high value on driving. That said, work commuters are more likely to switch to public transportation—especially to rail, which is usually less affected by traffic congestion—if the available transit alternatives are convenient to workplaces and commuting routes.

Expected Effects of Higher Gasoline Prices

Recent empirical research suggests that total driving, or vehicle miles traveled (VMT), is not currently very responsive to the price of gasoline. A 10 percent increase in gasoline prices is estimated to reduce VMT by as little as 0.2 percent to 0.3 percent in the short run and by 1.1 percent to 1.5 percent eventually.[1] A 2003 study of corporate average fuel economy (CAFE) standards, published by the National Research Council, cited slightly older estimates of the responsiveness of VMT to fuel costs that ranged from about 1 percent to 2 percent.[2]

Some of the VMT response comes from drivers who switch to commuter rail. An increase in gasoline prices raises the relative cost of driving compared with rail transit. As an illustration—in the opposite direction—of the price sensitivity of the demand for rail transit, a 10 percent increase in transit fares is estimated to reduce ridership by about 5 percent in the short run and by about 10 percent in the long run.[3] Survey research has indicated that a change in the cost of driving is the most important factor motorists consider when deciding whether to continue to drive or to switch to some other mode of transportation.[4] CBO's findings suggest, however, that a large increase in the price of gasoline might cause only a small shift from automobiles to public transportation, at least in the short run.

CBO's analysis is based on traffic volume (total vehicles per day) on metropolitan highways, rather than on total vehicle miles traveled. Those measures should be correlated, however: A general decline in VMT should reduce the volume of highway traffic, and most of that traffic occurs in metropolitan areas.[5] However, because recent research indicates that VMT is relatively insensitive to gasoline prices, the higher prices of the past several years should not be expected to cause large changes in freeway traffic volume.

When faced with an increase in gasoline prices, motorists should most readily curtail their lowest value trips. If they consider weekend trips generally less important than weekday trips, then weekend traffic volumes should be more sensitive to the price of gasoline. (CBO has no information about how weekday driving is valued compared with weekend driving.) However, freeway traffic volume should be more responsive to changing gasoline prices in places where transit rail service is available, particularly on weekdays. That is because rail service is probably a better substitute for weekday driving to work than it is for weekend driving, when transit service often is less frequent, some destinations (such as sports fields or places of worship) may be less well served by public transportation, and trips are more likely to involve hauling purchased items or recreational gear. The relative sensitivity of weekend versus weekday traffic to the price of gasoline ultimately is an empirical question, which is addressed by CBO's analysis.

Findings

Average weekday traffic volumes on some freeways have declined slightly in response to higher gasoline prices, CBO's analysis shows. The routes on which that response was detected are adjacent to commuter rail systems. Weekly average gasoline prices appear to have had little effect on traffic volume at other freeway locations or on weekends.[6] In the California data that CBO analyzed, higher gasoline prices also are associated with slightly greater ridership on transit rail systems.

The data consist of daily traffic counts for a dozen diverse freeway locations in metropolitan areas of California. The data cover the period from early 2003 through the end of 2006 and come from the state's four primary metropolitan areas (Sacramento, the San Francisco Bay Area, Los Angeles and Orange County, and San Diego County). For each area, CBO collected data at representative freeway locations adjacent to the commuter rail system in that region and at other locations in the region where rail transit was not available. (The figures and tables in Appendix A give details on the data.)

On average, over all locations, the price of gasoline in a given week had a negligible effect on the volume of weekend traffic, but on weekdays, higher gasoline prices had a small but statistically significant effect (see Table 1-1). A 20 percent increase in price, or 50 cents if the base price is $2.50 per gallon, would reduce weekday freeway traffic by an average of 0.4 percent. The effect would occur entirely in the response at rail-accessible freeway locations (as shown in the last two rows of the table). At those places, a 20 percent price increase would reduce weekday traffic by an average of 0.69 percent. That result is strongly statistically significant, although it amounts only to about 730 fewer vehicles out of an average of more than 106,000 vehicles per weekday at those locations. Gasoline prices did not affect weekend traffic volume at any of the locations, nor did they affect weekday traffic counts where rail commuting was not an option.[7]

Table 1-1. Estimated Effect of a 20 Percent Increase in Gasoline Price on Relative Traffic Volume

(Percent)		
	Weekends	**Weekdays**
Average Effect,		
All Sampled Routes	0.12	-0.40
Statistical Significance	Not significant	1.4 percent*
No Rail Option	0	0
Statistical Significance	Not significant	Not significant
Parallel Rail	0.20	-0.69
Statistical Significance	Not significant	0.04 percent**

Source: Congressional Budget Office based on data from the Freeway Performance Measurement Project, https://pems.eecs.berkeley.edu.

Notes: * = significant at <5 percent; ** = significant at <1 percent.

A 20 percent increase would be 50 cents per gallon if gasoline costs $2.50 per gallon or 60 cents if the price is $3.00.

The weekday response for rail-accessible freeway routes implies a traffic volume elasticity of -0.035 with respect to the price of gasoline. That result is roughly consistent with the short-run VMT elasticity estimate of -0.03 noted earlier, although that estimate represents all driving, not just driving on rail-accessible freeways. However, both elasticities indicate that gasoline prices have had a measurable, although small, effect on total driving.

Relationship between Traffic Volumes and Rail Ridership

Reductions in traffic volume correspond closely to increases in transit ridership. CBO analyzed monthly ridership totals for the municipal light-rail systems in Sacramento, Los Angeles, and San Diego and for the subway systems in Los Angeles and the San Francisco Bay Area. (In order to combine the data from different-sized transit systems into the same analysis, CBO expressed each system's ridership as a percentage of its average in a baseline period—the same treatment it applied to freeway traffic volumes.) Adjusting for long-term ridership trends on each system, seasonal effects, and inertia (the tendency for ridership totals to persist from one month to the next), CBO estimates that the same increase of 20 percent in gasoline prices that affects freeway traffic volume is associated with an increase of 1.9 percent in average system ridership. That result is moderately statistically significant: It can be asserted with 95 percent confidence that higher gasoline prices are associated with increased ridership.

For an average-sized system, that result translates into about 1,870 additional rail trips per day in each direction, throughout the system.[8] For a transit system that has several branches running alongside freeways—as the systems in CBO's sample have—that implies an additional 625 to 935 riders per line for systems with, respectively, three or two such lines. Thus, as gasoline prices have increased, the average number of riders gained by the rail transit systems in CBO's sample has been reasonably consistent with the reduction in the number of vehicles per weekday, about 730, on the adjacent freeways. In CBO's analysis, all five transit systems exhibited positive relationships between ridership and gasoline prices, although for the two (interconnected) Los Angeles systems, the effect was small and not statistically different from zero.

SPEED OF TRAFFIC

Another way that motorists can reduce their fuel costs is to drive more slowly. The incentive to slow down will depend on how much gasoline prices have increased, how much fuel would be saved by slowing down, and how much motorists value their time while driving. The value of the potential fuel savings from slowing down is rather small compared with reasonable measures of many motorists' value of time, so the likely effect of gasoline prices on highway speeds also should be rather small. For any given reduction in speed, however, the fuel savings are greater at faster speeds and for less-fuelefficient vehicles.

The development of freeway congestion-pricing projects—which charge tolls that rise with the amount of traffic congestion—has enabled researchers to estimate motorists' value of time during congested commuting hours. Estimates for California's high-occupancy toll lanes along State Route 91, west of Riverside, and Interstate 15, north of San Diego, indicate, on the basis of tolls and travel time savings in toll lanes versus free lanes, that motorists value their time between $20 and $45 per hour of reduced travel time.[9]

In other contexts, where toll-based estimates are not available, economists typically use average hourly after- tax wage rates as a proxy for motorists' value of time.[10] Consistent with that, motorists' preferred driving speeds have been found to be positively associated with income.[11]

There have been studies that link driving speeds and motorists' value of time, but CBO's analysis is among the few published studies on the relationship between driving speeds and *gasoline prices.* Previous work, now decades old, also found a link between higher gasoline prices and slower driving.[12] And new research has identified a relationship between higher gasoline prices and lower motor vehicle fatality rates, although the researchers attributed it to a reduction in vehicle miles traveled and did not consider whether slower driving also could have contributed to the decline in fatalities.[13]

In response to higher gasoline prices, drivers optimally would slow just to the speed at which the value of the fuel saved equaled the value of time lost to slower driving. By that logic, motorists who valued their time more would slow down less, or not at all, than drivers who valued their time at a lower rate per hour. At any given gasoline price, a motorist's preferred speed also depends on factors that are unrelated to gasoline prices or the value of time, such as the local speed limit and its enforcement, the time of day, the time of year, the physical characteristics of the road at that location, and traffic density.[14] However, in keeping with the evidence cited earlier, speed should be correlated with the value that motorists place on their time.

BOX 1-1. EMPIRICAL RESULTS AND THE VALUE OF TIME AND SAFETY

If the speeds at which motorists drive are positively correlated with how much they value their time, then a disproportionate number of slower-driving motorists would have lower-than-average values of time and faster-driving motorists would have higher values.[1] If that is the case, then the findings of the Congressional Budget Office (CBO) about the effects of the price of gasoline on highway speeds are consistent with the prediction that motorists with lower values of time will be more responsive to an increase in gasoline prices than will drivers with higher values of time. (CBO has no information about whether driving speeds and values of time are correlated.) The results also could be explained if all motorists have a similar distribution of driving speeds and a similar response to gasoline prices, or if drivers of less-fuelefficient vehicles tend to drive more slowly than do drivers whose vehicles get better mileage. However, those explanations would require that all motorists value their time about the same. Given the wide variation in motorists' effective wage rates, that premise seems unlikely.

If different motorists do have different propensities to drive faster or slower, the findings also imply that higher gasoline prices increase the variance in high-way driving speeds at a given time. That would mean more interactions, such as passing. In that case, motorists who wish to maintain a given level of safety would need to devote slightly more attention to tasks such as monitoring other vehicles and maintaining their desired following distance.[2] However, because higher gasoline prices also would cause drivers to reduce vehicle speeds slightly, the effect on safety is indeterminate but probably negligible because the changes in speed are small.

---

[1] One useful way of thinking about the concept of motorists' value of time is the amount they would be willing to pay to reduce their travel time by one hour.

[2] For a discussion of the possibility of a negative link between variance of speed and highway safety, see Charles A. Lave, "Speeding, Coordination, and the 55-MPH Limit," *American Economic Review,* vol. 75, no. 5 (1985), pp. 1159–1 164; and Theodore E. Keeler, "Highway Safety, Economic Behavior, and Driving Environment," *American Economic Review,* vol. 84, no. 3 (1994), pp. 684–693.

CBO's analytical results are consistent with that observation. In all likelihood, few if any motorists know what their optimal response should be (with respect to driving speed) when gasoline prices change. But CBO's analysis suggests that drivers' responses may be proportionate to their value of time. That is, if motorists can be said to have particular speed preferences, then those who tended to drive more slowly than average before gasoline prices increased appear to have slowed slightly more than other drivers did, and faster drivers have not reduced their speeds at all.[15] Overall, as described with the rest of the findings, the amount of fuel saved as a result is consistent with recent estimates of the price elasticity of the demand for gasoline (The variation in motorists' driving speeds as a response to higher gasoline prices may have some implication for highway safety; see Box 1-1.).

How Much Slowing Is "Sensible" When Fuel Prices Rise?

A study conducted by Oak Ridge National Laboratory (ORNL) showed that slowing from 70 miles per hour (mph) to 65 mph—a 7.1 percent reduction—would reduce a typical vehicle's fuel consumption from 3.7 to 3.4 gallons per 100 miles, an 8.2 percent reduction. At $3 per gallon, the fuel savings would be worth 0.9 cents per mile. Travel time would increase by about 4 seconds per mile.[16]

Figure 1-1 shows the average relationship between speed and fuel consumption for speeds from 15 mph to 75 mph.

Table 1-2 is based on the data underlying Figure 1-1. It shows average fuel savings per hour of additional travel time caused by slower driving, compared with the fuel and time consumed when driving at 70 mph. For example, when the price of gasoline is $2.50 per gallon, slowing from 70 mph to 69 mph would generate fuel savings of $7.47 for every hour "lost" to slower driving. Thus, for motorists who value their time at less than $7.47 per hour—and who would prefer to drive 70 mph or faster if gasoline were less expensive—the value of fuel saved by slowing to 69 mph would exceed the cost in terms of additional travel time. For drivers who value their time at more than $7.47 per hour, the financial benefit of slowing would be less than the time cost.

(Gallons per hundred miles)

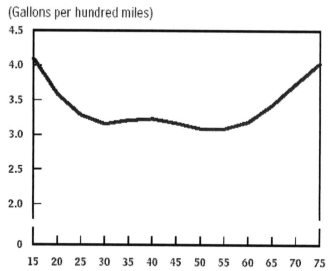

Source: Congressional Budget Office based on data from the Bureau of Transportation Statistics. See Stacy C. Davis, *Transportation Energy Data Book: Edition 21-2001*, ORNL-6966 (prepared by Oak Ridge National Laboratory for the Department of Energy Office of Transportation Technologies, October 2001), www.ornl.gov/~webworks/cppr/ y2001/rpt/111858.pdf, Tables 7.21 and 7.22; B.H. West and others, *Development and Validation of Light-Duty Modal Emissions and Fuel Consumption Values for Traffic Models*, FHWA-RD-99-068 (Federal Highway Administration, 1999).

Note: The results are based on nine representative vehicles selected and tested by Oak Ridge National Laboratory.

Figure 1-1. Fuel Consumption and Vehicle Speed.

More generally, Table 1-2 suggests that an increase in the price of gasoline will cause some motorists, but not all, to slow down when they are driving on uncongested free-ways For example, no motorist with a value of time above $10.45 per hour and a preference for driving 70 mph would slow down as long as the price of gasoline remained below $3.50 per gallon. The table also suggests that a motorist's optimal response should vary inversely with that motorist's value of time. For example, if the price of a gallon of gasoline rose from $2.50 to $3.00, a motorist who prefers to drive 70 mph would slow by anywhere from 1 mph to 10 mph for values of time ranging from around $9 per hour to below $7 per hour, respectively. In September 2005, when the price of gasoline first reached $3 per gallon in

California, the median after-tax wage rate in that state was $11.27 per hour—close enough to the values in Table 1-2 that the price should have caused motorists to drive more slowly if their value of time was several dollars (or more) below the statewide median wage.[17]

It would be difficult to detect the effect of gasoline prices on speeds in heavy traffic, because motorists already must drive more slowly than they prefer in such conditions. For that reason, CBO analyzed driving speeds only for weekends, when freeways are demonstrably less congested than they are on weekdays.[18] If motorists value their time less on the weekends, their weekend driving speeds also should be more sensitive to gasoline prices. Thus, if no slowdown could be detected in weekend driving, probably none could be detected in weekday travel either.

Table 1-2. Value of Fuel Saved by Slowing from 70 Miles Per Hour, as a Function of the Price of Gasoline

(Dollars)				Time Lost (Seconds)		
Price per Gallon	Fuel Cost per Mile[a]	Target Speed (Miles per hour)	Value of Fuel Saved per Mile[b]	Per Mile	Per Penny Saved	Savings per Hour[c]
2.50	0.093	69	0.0015	0.75	4.9	7.47
		69	0.0019	0.75	4.0	8.96
3.00	0.112	65	0.0092	3.96	4.3	8.37
		60	0.0164	8.57	5.2	6.89
3.50	0.131	69	0.0022	0.75	3.4	10.45

Source: Congressional Budget Office based on Oak Ridge National Laboratory (ORNL) estimates of average fuel consumption versus speed.

a. At 70 miles per hour (mph) and at a given gasoline price, under ORNL's assumption of an average of 26.8 miles per gallon at 70 mph.

b. At target speed compared with 70 mph. Value determined by gasoline price times the quantity of fuel saved.

c. Value of fuel savings per hour of lost time (not clock time). At 65 mph, 4 minutes and 37 seconds of travel time is lost per hour of clock time, compared with the amount of travel time at 70 mph.

Findings

Higher gasoline prices from 2003 through the end of 2006 caused many motorists to drive a little more slowly on uncongested highways. Median speeds in free-flow conditions declined slightly as gasoline prices increased. The slowdown was more pronounced for vehicles moving at the somewhat lower 5th percentile speeds; there was no discernible effect on 95th percentile speeds. The median effect is consistent with recent estimates of gasoline price elasticity, which indicate that short-run demand declines by around 0.6 percent when the price rises by 10 percent, all else being equal.[19] The diverse effects of gasoline prices on vehicles traveling at different speeds are consistent with the notion that motorists who set a lower value on their time may be more willing to trade (slightly) longer travel times for (slightly) lower fuel costs.

The data CBO examined consist of distributions (percentile values) of weekend vehicle speeds over a month, with a separate distribution for each hour of day and each month.[20] CBO collected data for three locations, recording each month's 5th, 50th (median), and 95th percentile weekend speeds at each location for each hour of the day. Table 1-3 reports sample statistics for those data and median traffic volumes for each location. Interstate 405 in Orange County is the busiest of the three sampled locations, with a median volume of 5,530 vehicles per hour over the entire sample.[21] That location also has the slowest 5th percentile speeds, averaging 59 mph over all hours of the day, compared with a little less than 63 mph on I-680 in San Ramon and nearly 67 mph on I8 in San Diego. Median speeds are more similar across the three locations, ranging from 66.4 mph to 69.5 mph, on average. The averages in Table 1-3 include some congested traffic; as described in the appendix, data that appear to indicate congested travel were excluded from the analysis.

From 2003 to 2006, the monthly average (nominal) price of gasoline doubled, from $1.66 to a peak of $3.34 in May 2006. Over that time, average nominal hourly wages rose by only 11 percent, from $15.36 to $17.02 per hour.[22]

For this study, CBO developed a statistical model of driving speed as a function of the price of gasoline and other factors, including seasonal and freeway-specific effects. Holding those other factors constant, the model indicates that a 50 cent increase in the price of gasoline would cause median freeway speeds in the sample to decline by a little more than three-quarters of a mile per hour. (For example, at the study's mean gasoline price of $2.35 per gallon and the median freeway speed of 67.8 mph on uncongested freeways, when the price of gasoline reached $2.85 per gallon, the median speed would have declined, on average, to 67.0 mph.) The effect on slower vehicles is 50 percent greater: Fifth percentile speeds would decline by about 1.2 mph. By contrast, higher gasoline prices do not appear to have affected 95th percentile speeds: Faster- moving traffic appears not to have slowed down as gasoline prices increased, at least over the period observed in the data (see Table 1-4 on page 12).

The median result translates into an elasticity of speed of about -0.05 with respect to the real price of gasoline— which is to say that a 10 percent increase in the price of gasoline would cause the median speed to decline by about 0.5 percent. That result, applied to the findings of the ORNL study, implies that for an average vehicle driven at highway speed, fuel consumption would decline by about 1.2 percent, or slightly less than one-twentieth of a gallon per 100 miles. Those savings—a teaspoon of gasoline every 2.6 miles—imply a gasoline demand elasticity in urban highway driving of about -0.06 with respect to the price of gasoline.

Table 1-3. Average Weekend Speeds on Three California Highways, 2003 to 2006

(Miles per hour)	I-680 (North) San amon	I-405 (South) Orange County	I-8 (West) San Diego
Median Number of Vehicles per Hour	3,460	5,530	3,620
5th Percentile Speed	62.7	59.0	66.8
Median Speed	66.4	67.6	69.5
95th Percentile Speed	70.3	70.9	71.3

Source: Congressional Budget Office based on data from the Freeway Performance Measurement Project, https://pems.eecs.berkeley.edu.

Notes: I = Interstate.

Excluding 1 a.m to 6 a.m. In the bottom three rows, each figure is the average of the given percentile speed in each month for each hour on Saturdays and Sundays. With 19 hours between 6 a.m. and 1 a.m., each figure is an average of 48 months × 19 hours = 912 values.

Table 1-4. Estimated Effect of a 50 Cent Increase in the Price of Gasoline on Highway Speeds

	5th Percentile	Median	95th Percentile
Baseline Speed (mph)	62.8	67.8	70.8
Change in Speed (mph)	- 1.2 [**]	- 0.8 [**]	No change
Elasticity of Speed with Respect to the Price of Gasoline	-0.09	-0.05	0
Implied Elasticity of Fuel Consumption[a]	-0.08	-0.06	0

Source: Congressional Budget Office based on data from the Freeway Performance Measurement Project, https://pems.eecs.berkeley.edu.

Note: mph = miles per hour; ** = significant at 1 percent. The differences between effects also are significant at 1 percent.

a. Estimate applies to an average vehicle traveling at baseline speed. Total gasoline price elasticity would reflect additional types of adjustments.

Thus, along with conventionally understood sources of elasticity in the demand for gasoline—changes in the length and frequency of automobile trips and in the types of vehicles people drive—the way vehicles are operated could be a meaningful source of short-run elasticity in the demand for gasoline. In particular, although the implied elasticity of -0.06 is objectively small, it is consistent with current estimates of the overall short-run elasticity, which range from about -0.03 to -0.09.[23]

The analysis of driving speeds shows that if gasoline costs $2.85 per gallon, motorists with average fuel economy vehicles who slow from the median speed by 0.75 mph would cut their fuel expenditures by about 0.13 cents per mile. Those savings would accumulate at a rate of about $8 per hour of *additional* travel time—about 30 percent less than the median hourly after-tax wage rate for California in 2005.[24] At the 5th percentile speed, slowing by 1.2 mph would cut fuel expenditures by about 0.16 cents per mile, or about $5.24 per additional hour of travel time compared with the baseline speed of 62.8 mph. Motorists who travel at the 95th percentile speed, and who do not slow in response to higher gasoline prices, would be implicitly valuing their driving time at $8.60 per hour or more.[25] (Another way motorists can reduce the per-mile cost of driving is to switch to a lower grade of gasoline; see Box 1-2).

BOX 1-2. DECLINING PURCHASES OF MIDGRADE AND PREMIUM GASOLINE

Higher gasoline prices have induced many drivers to make small changes in the way they operate their vehicles. The higher prices also may have caused some consumers to switch to lower octane formulations, which generally are sold at slightly lower prices. There currently tends to be a difference of about 20 cents per gallon between the prices of regular and premium gasoline; the price for midgrade gasoline tends to fall in the middle.[1]

Anecdotal evidence suggests that some consumers are satisfied with their vehicles' performance using a lower octane gasoline than that recommended by the manufacturer. As gasoline prices rise, consumers may become more willing to ignore manufacturers' recommendations and switch to a less expensive grade of gasoline. It is also the case, however, that if the price of each grade increases by the same amount, the *relative* price of the higher grade *falls* in comparison to the price for each lower grade. That shift can cause some consumers to substitute toward a higher grade, although the empirical evidence for that phenomenon is mixed and rather sparse.[2] In either case, given the low elasticity of overall demand for gasoline, grade switching has little effect on total U.S. gasoline consumption.

Consumption of midgrade and premium gasoline has been declining in absolute terms since 2000 (see the accompanying figure); consumption of regular fuel has increased. Some of the decline in the use of higher octane fuels might reflect a change in vehicle designs and in sales of vehicles that require higher grades of gasoline. However, as with grade switching, the Congressional Budget Office did not analyze the extent to which changing engine designs and consumer preferences have contributed to the decline in sales of higher octane fuels.

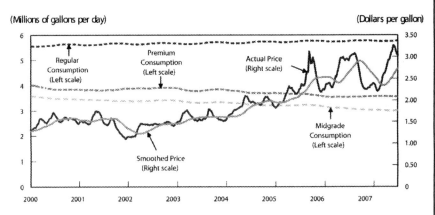

Source: Congressional Budget Office based on data from the Department of Energy, Energy Information Administration.

Notes: Prices are nominal at-the-pump prices and include all taxes, ending in May 2007. The smoothed price series is a six-month moving average, computed by CBO. Consumption totals were converted to logarithms (left scale) by CBO.

Retail Prices and Consumption of Gasoline

[1] In 2006, the U.S. average prices for regular and premium grades were $2.59 and $2.80 per gallon, respectively. See Department of Energy, Energy Information Administration, *Monthly Energy Review* (October 2007), p. 132, Table 9.4, Motor Gasoline Retail Prices, U.S. City Average, *www.eia.doe.gov/emeu/ mer/pdf/pages/sec9_6.pdf.*

[2] See Robert Lawson and Lauren Raymer, "Testing the Alchian–Allen Theorem: A Study of Consumer Behavior in the Gasoline Market," *Economics Bulletin,* vol. 4, issue 35 (2006), pp. 1–6, http://economicsbulletin.vanderbilt.edu/ 2006/volume4/ EB-06D00021A.pdf; and Todd M. Nesbit, *Excise Taxation and Product Quality: The Gasoline Market,* Working Paper 05-11 (Morgantown: West Virginia University, Department of Economics, 2005), www.be.wvu.edu/ div/econ//work/ pdf_files/05-11 .pdf.

The theorem was originally explained by Armen Alchian and William Allen in *Exchange and Production: Competition, Coordination, and Control* (Belmont, Calif.: Wadsworth, 1983; originally published as *University Economics: Elements of Inquiry,* 1964) and further developed by Yoram Barzel in "An Alternative Approach to Analysis and Taxation," *Journal of Political Economy,* vol. 84, no. 6 (1976), pp. 1177–1197.

Such small responses are unlikely to result from conscious calculations. Few motorists would have the information required to gauge their responses so acutely, nor the time or inclination to do so. However, higher prices make drivers pay more attention to speed. The modest reductions in speed suggest that drivers may have responded by easing off slightly on the gasoline pedal or dialing back cruise-control settings a notch. If only a minority of drivers have that response, their reduced speeds could cause nearby drivers to slow down as well, even if gasoline prices alone would not have that effect. Both kinds of response contribute to elasticity in the demand for gasoline.

APPLICABILITY OF FINDINGS TO OTHER REGIONS OF THE UNITED STATES

Although they are based on California data, the findings of this study are more or less applicable to other, similar metropolitan areas in the United States. Motorist populations, highway and mass transit infrastructure, and vehicle stocks differ somewhat from one part of the country to another, and gasoline prices vary from state to state because of differences in state taxes and regional supply.[26] Retail gasoline prices tend to be higher in California not only because gasoline pipelines that serve many other parts of the country do not extend into California but also because the gasoline sold in that state's metropolitan areas is reformulated as required by the Clean Air Act, adding about three cents to the retail price.[27] Despite the differences, changes in gasoline prices tend to be highly correlated, so consumers throughout the country have had similar financial incentives to reduce their consumpion of gasoline.[28] This study's findings on highway speeds may be more generally applicable than are its findings on the volume of traffic, which apply to areas served by rail transit systems.

Higher gasoline prices could have a smaller effect on VMT in rural areas, in California or elsewhere, because there are fewer alternatives to driving and because trip distances may be greater. However, the largest share of total VMT occurs on highways in metropolitan areas.[29] This study's findings on vehicle speeds in urban highway driving may, if anything, understate the effect of higher gasoline prices on driving speeds in rural areas because median household income—and presumably motorists' valuation of their time—tends to be considerably higher in urban areas.[30]

End Notes

[1] The VMT effect is slightly smaller, therefore, than the more general effect of gasoline prices on the demand for gasoline, estimated in recent research to be about -0.6. See Kenneth A. Small and Kurt Van Dender, "Fuel Efficiency and Motor Vehicle Travel: The Declining Rebound Effect," *Energy Journal*, vol. 28, no. 1 (2007), pp. 25–51. Other estimates of VMT elasticity (in the literature reviewed in that study) were higher, ranging from -0.10 to -0.16 in the short run and -0.26 to -0.31 in the long run. Small and Van Dender's estimates are based on recent data, and they attribute their estimates' being lower than those in the reviewed literature to growth of real (inflation-adjusted) income and lower real fuel prices, which have combined to make the cost of driving a smaller share of personal disposable income.

[2] Technically, what is estimated is the VMT *elasticity* with respect to fuel costs, or the percentage change in VMT that results from a 1 percent change in per-mile fuel costs. See National Research Council, *Effectiveness and Impact of Corporate Average Fuel Economy (CAFE) Standards* (Washington, D.C.: National Academy Press, 2002), available from www.nap.edu/ catalog.php?record_id=10172. For VMT elasticity estimates, that report cites David L. Greene, James Kahn, and R. Gibson, "Fuel Economy Rebound Effect for U.S. Household Vehicles," *Energy Journal*, vol. 20, no. 3 (1999), pp. 1–31; J. Haughton and S. Sarker, "Gasoline Tax as a Corrective Tax: Estimates for the United States. 1970–1991," *Energy Journal*, vol. 17, no. 2 (1996), pp. 103–126; and C.T. Jones, "Another Look at U.S. Passenger Vehicle Use and the 'Rebound' Effect from Improved Fuel Efficiency," *Energy Journal*, vol. 14, no. 4 (1993), pp. 99–110.

[3] Richard Voith, "Fares, Service Levels, and Demographics: What Determines Commuter Rail Ridership in the Long Run?" *Journal of Urban Economics*, vol. 41 (1997), pp. 176–197. In earlier research, Voith reported a somewhat lower elasticity of ridership; see "The Long-Run Elasticity of Commuter Rail Demand," *Journal of Urban Economics*, vol. 30 (1991), pp. 360–372.

[4] The primary costs considered in the survey were tolls and parking charges, but gasoline prices also affect driving costs. Lesser factors included increases in the time to drive a given distance and improvements in the quality of other modes of transportation. See Kevin Washbrook, Wolfgang Haider, and Mark Jaccard, "Estimating Commuter Mode Choice: A Discrete Choice Analysis of the Impact of Road Pricing and Parking Charges," *Transportation,* vol. 33, no. 6 (2006), pp. 621–639.

[5] The correlation would be lower to the extent that the reduction in VMT attributable to higher gasoline prices occurred less on metropolitan highways and more on surface streets or rural highways. (That would be the case, for example, if urban-area residents responded to higher gasoline prices by cutting back on their out- of-town highway travel.)

[6] CBO's sample did not include rural highways. A decline in out-of- town automobile travel, such as weekend recreational trips, would not necessarily be detectable in the data used for this analysis.

[7] Some results in Table 1-1 are sensitive to the inclusion of a location on eastbound Interstate 80 that often carries significant weekend recreational traffic toward Lake Tahoe. With I-80 in the sample, the "no rail option" weekend response is positive (indicating *more* driving in response to higher gasoline prices) and statistically significant, suggesting that the model is misspecified (in particular, it lacks indicator variables for weekends in summer and in ski season).

[8] The systems in CBO's sample averaged about 4.1 million trips per month in 2006, ranging from 8.8 million on Bay Area Rapid Transit to 1.2 million on Sacramento's light-rail system. Thus, 1.9 percent translates to about 78,000 additional trips per month, or 1,870 trips per (nonholiday) weekday, under an assumption that each added rider takes two trips (one round-trip) per day— 21 days a month, on average.

[9] The range of values is attributable to differences in the commuter populations on the two freeways. The estimates may slightly overstate true values of time, as they may also reflect motorists' willingness to pay for greater reliability and perceived safer conditions on toll roads. See David Brownstone and others, "Drivers' Willingness-to-Pay to Reduce Travel Time: Evidence from the San Diego I-15 Congestion Pricing Project," *Transportation Research, Part A: Policy and Practice,* vol. 37 (2003), pp. 372–3 87. For results from SR-9 1 in Riverside, see Kenneth A. Small, Clifford Winston, and Jia Yan, "Uncovering the Distribution of Motorists' Preferences for Travel Time and Reliability," *Econometrica,* vol. 73, no. 4 (2005), pp. 1367–1382.

[10] On the basis of his review of the economic literature, Kenneth Small concluded that "a reasonable average value of time for the journey to work is 50 percent of the [motorist's] gross wage rate." See Kenneth A. Small, *Urban Transportation Economics,* vol. 51 of *Fundamentals of Pure and Applied Economics* (Newark, N.J.: Harwood Academic Publishers, 1992), p. 44. For value-of-time estimates not based on road tolls, see Orley Ashenfelter and Michael Greenstone, "Using Mandated Speed Limits to Measure the Value of a Statistical Life," *Journal of Political Economy,* vol. 112, no. 1 (2004), pp. S226–S267. See also Robert T. Deacon and Jon Sonstelie, "Rationing by Waiting and the Value of Time: Results from a Natural Experiment," *Journal of Political Economy,* vol. 93, no. 1 (1985), pp. 627–647. Deacon and Sonstelie report that drivers who voluntarily queued for lower- priced gasoline implicitly valued their waiting time at amounts similar to their after-tax wages. Finally, a long-ago survey of empirical studies of choices of commuting modes showed that, on average, the estimated value of time spent commuting was only about 20 percent to 30 percent of wages, although that analysis examined commuting by all modes of transit, not just private automobiles. See Nils Bruzelius, *The Value of Travel Time: Theory and Measurement* (London: Croom Helm, 1979).

[11] Young-Jun Kweon and Kara Kockelman, "Driver Attitudes and Choices: Speed Limits, Seat Belt Use, and Drinking-andDriving," *Journal of Transportation Research Forum,* vol. 45, no. 3 (2006), pp. 39–56.

[12] A 1979 report (based on 1972 data) found that a 10 percent increase in gasoline prices would have induced a 3.5 percent decrease in annual statewide average highway speeds. See Carol A. Dahl, "Consumer Adjustment to a Gasoline Tax," *Review of Economics and Statistics,* vol. 61, no. 3 (1979), pp. 427–432. More-recent work finds a weak (not statistically significant) link between higher gasoline prices and slower speeds (Nicholas E. Burger and Daniel T. Kaffine, "Gas Prices, Traffic, and Freeway Speeds in Los Angeles," University of California at Santa Barbara, Department of Economics, unpublished working paper). The lack of significance may stem from a failure to account for correlations in highway speeds along different routes and at different times and in considering speeds only within a pair of two-hour nighttime periods.

[13] See David Grabowski and Michael Morrisey, "Do Higher Gasoline Taxes Save Lives?" *Economics Letters,* vol. 90 (2006), pp. 5 1–55. A more in-depth exposition of that research—albeit with a focus on declining real gasoline prices—appears in Grabowski and Morrisey, "Gasoline Prices and Motor Vehicle Fatalities," *Journal of Policy Analysis and Management,* vol. 23, no. 3 (2004), pp. 575–593.

[14] Those factors are accounted for in CBO's analysis. Weather and daylight conditions can greatly influence speed; the analysis does not explicitly control for those factors, but they are correlated with seasons, which the analysis does consider.

[15] CBO does not have data on individual motorists, so it is not possible to determine the extent to which individual drivers tend to drive faster or more slowly nor to observe differences in how such motorists respond to gasoline prices. However, CBO's findings are consistent with that suggestion.

[16] See B.H. West and others, *Development and Validation of Light- Duty Modal Emissions and Fuel Consumption Values for Traffic Models,* FHWA-RD-99-068 (Federal Highway Administration, 1999).

[17] The California Energy Commission tracks weekly gasoline prices; see www.energy PRESENT.XLS. According to the Bureau of Labor Statistics, in 2005, the median hourly wage rate for all occupations, including salaried positions, was $15.80 in California (archived data; see ftp://ftp.bls.gov/pub/special.requests/cew/2005/state/; for current values, see www.bls.gov/oes/current/oes_ca.htm); the national median wage was nearly the same. Thus, the median after-tax wage rate would have been $11.27, on the basis of a marginal tax rate of 28.65 percent (15 percent for federal income tax, 7.65 percent for Social Security and Medicare payroll tax, and 6 percent for state income tax). For an analysis of effective tax rates, allowing for deductions, see Congressional Budget Office, *Effective Marginal Tax Rates on Labor Income* (November 2005). See also California Franchise Tax Board, 2006 California Tax Table, www.ftb.ca.gov/forms/06_forms/06_540tt.pdf.

[18] CBO's comparison of weekend and weekday freeway speeds at all sampled locations revealed significant regular slowdowns during weekday commutes that did not occur in weekend traffic.

[19] The 0.6 percent represents the midpoint of a range of recent estimates. Jonathan E. Hughes, Christopher R. Knittel, and Daniel Sperling, *Evidence of a Shift in the Short-Run Price Elasticity of Gasoline Demand,* Research Report UCD-ITS-RR-06-16 (University of California, Davis: Institute of Transportation Studies, 2006), estimate that the short-run demand elasticity for gasoline ranges between about -0.3 and -0.8; for Small and Van Dender, "Fuel Efficiency and Motor Vehicle Travel," the range of estimates is from about -0.5 to -0.9.

[20] A distribution is, in effect, a continuous histogram that describes the complete range of observed vehicle speeds and the frequency with which they are observed. That information is reported as percentile values: For example, the 5th percentile or 50th percentile (median) speeds are those faster than, respectively, the speeds at which 5 percent or 50 percent of the vehicles were driven.

[21] Each location has four lanes in each direction; I-405 in Orange County also has a fifth, HOV (high-occupancy vehicle) lane, but its traffic flow and speed data are not included in CBO's

sample. Median traffic volumes in Table 1-3 are for one direction, for hours from 6 a.m. through 1 a.m.

[22] Data on average gasoline prices come from the Department of Energy, Energy Information Administration; data on average hourly wages come from the Bureau of Labor Statistics.

[23] In "Fuel-Efficiency and Motor Vehicle Travel," Small and Van Dender used U.S. market data for 1997 to 2001 to estimate the elasticity of fuel consumption with respect to price at -0.066 (with a standard error of 0.01). They report that higher fuel costs (58 percent above the sample's average) yield a slightly higher elasticity (-0.074, with a standard error of 0.007). Hughes and his colleagues, in *Evidence of a Shift in the Short-Run Price Elasticity of Gasoline Demand,* estimate a range for short-run demand elasticity (on the basis of data from 2001 to 2006) of -0.034 to -0.077. See also Michael Morris, "Short-Run Motor Gasoline Demand Model" (presentation at the Energy Outlook, Modeling and Data Conference, Department of Energy, Energy Information Administration, Washington, D.C., March 28, 2007, www.eia.doe.gov/ oiaf/aeo/conf/pdf/morris.pdf). He estimates, on the basis of data from 1977 to 1989, that the short-run elasticity of demand for gasoline ranged from -0.05 to -0.08; data from 1994 to 2006 led to an estimate of -0.02 to -0.04.

[24] If a motorist slowed from 67.8 mph to 67 mph, it would take about 90 hours (and more than 6,000 miles) of driving to accumulate 1 hour of additional travel time.

[25] By comparison, Small and colleagues, in "Uncovering the Distribution of Motorists' Preferences," report that along California's SR-91 the median value of time for weekday morning commuters (4 a.m. to 10 a.m.) is $21.46 per hour, about 93 percent of the surveyed motorists' average wage rate. The 90 percent confidence interval around that estimate extends down to $11.47. That value is higher than CBO's statewide average value, perhaps because workers who accept the kinds of long-distance commutes that commuters along SR-9 1 have would tend to do so for jobs that pay higher wages.

[26] In 2006, California's state tax on gasoline was 40.1 cents per gallon, the nation's third highest gasoline tax. Nationwide, the average tax was 27.1 cents per gallon; New York's was highest (41.7 cents per gallon) and Alaska's was lowest (8 cents per gallon). See American Petroleum Institute, "Gasoline Taxes, October 2006," www.api.org/policy/tax/stateexcise/uploadoctober_2006_gasoline_and_diesel_summary_pa ges.pdf.

[27] For information about reformulated gasoline, see Environmental Protection Agency, *Gasoline Fuels, Reformulated Gasoline Emission Facts,* EPA420-F-99-040 (November 1999), www.epa.gov/otaq/ f99040.htm. According to data compiled by the American Automobile Association, average retail gasoline prices are often higher in California than in any other state (see www.fuelgaugereport.com/ sbsavg.asp for current statewide average prices). Hawaii also tends to have relatively high gasoline prices; Idaho, Wyoming, and Utah often have relatively low prices.

[28] See Department of Energy, Energy Information Administration, *U.S. Retail Gasoline Prices,* www.eia.doe.gov/oil data_publications/wrgp/mogas_home_page.html.

[29] Urban highways such as those in this study carry 35 percent of total VMT. Rural interstate highways and other highways ("principal arterials") carry about 18 percent of VMT. The remainder of VMT, in comparatively smaller shares, occurs on urban and rural "minor arterial" routes, collector roads, and local roads. See Marilouise Burgess, *Contrasting Rural and Urban Fatal Crashes, 1994–2003,* NHTSA Technical Report DOT HS 809 896 (National Highway Traffic Safety Administration, Department of Transportation, December 2005), www.nrd.nhtsa.dot.gov/Pubs/809896.PDF, Table 3, p. 19.

[30] The Census Bureau reported that in 2005 the median household income for metropolitan areas was $48,474, compared with $37,564 outside of those areas. See Carmen DeNavas-Walt, Bernadette D. Proctor, and Cheryl Hill Lee, *Income, Poverty, and Health Insurance Coverage in the United States: 2005,* Current Population Reports P60-231 (Bureau of the Census, August 2006), p. 6, Table 1, "Income and Earnings Summary Measures by Selected Characteristics: 2004 and 2005," www.census.gov/ prod/2006pubs/p60-23 1.pdf.

In: Gasoline Prices and their Effects on Behavior   ISBN: 978-1-60741-351-6
Editor: Hermann Schreiber   © 2010 Nova Science Publishers, Inc.

Chapter 2

GASOLINE PRICES AND VEHICLE MARKETS

Congressional Budget Office

The longer gasoline prices remain high, the broader the scope of actions consumers will take in response—in part because the longer high prices are sustained, the more they affect consumers' expectations about future prices. Those expectations influence consumers' longterm choices in several areas—including their decisions about what kinds of automobiles to drive and how many miles they are prepared to commute to work. All of those choices impinge on gasoline consumption and are in contrast to consumers' immediate, short-term, largely behavioral adjustments to high gasoline prices, which involve how fast or how much to drive, for example.

A shift in the kinds of vehicles consumers buy can affect overall gasoline consumption, but only gradually because many vehicles already in operation when the shift occurs remain in use for a dozen years or more. In contrast, signs of a shift can be detected relatively quickly in vehicle sales data, as was apparently the case with automobile sales after the average price of a gallon of gasoline first rose above $3, in September 2005. That price threshold was exceeded again in the spring and summer of 2006 and yet again through much of 2007. Since 2005, the sale of cars relative to light trucks has increased, after declining for several decades. After stagnating for a comparable period, the average fuel economy of new cars has increased, as has that for light trucks.

Whether those effects will be sustained in future vehicle model years depends on whether real gasoline prices remain substantially above their historic average, how those prices affect automakers' future product decisions and the demand for those products, and how quickly consumers' real income grows in relation to the growth in their fuel costs of driving. If gasoline prices drop back to earlier levels, the effect of high prices on the overall passenger vehicle fleet might be limited to vehicles sold while consumers expected gasoline prices to remain high. If high gasoline prices persist, however, and if consumers continue to respond as they have in the past few years, the composition of the passenger vehicle fleet eventually could resemble that of the vehicles sold in the 2005 and 2006 model years, as described below.

Some of the recent decline in market share for light trucks could be attributable to the imposition of stricter fuel economy standards for those vehicles, which include crossover and sport–utility vehicles (SUVs).[1] The new standards could have led to price or attribute changes in some light-truck models that induced some consumers to purchase cars instead. The phase-out of some of the favorable tax treatment for business use of light trucks also could have changed some companies' buying patterns. Some tax benefit is still provided for those purchases, however, and the effect of the phased-out benefit may not have been large.[2] Still, the contribution of either factor to the loss in the light-truck market share remains uncertain.

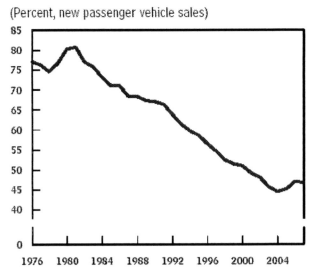

(Percent, new passenger vehicle sales)

Source: Congressional Budget Office based on data from the Bureau of Economic Analysis.

Figure 2-1. Market Share of Cars versus Light Trucks, 1976 to 2007.

The relationship between gasoline prices and the demand for automobiles was the subject of several economic studies in the 1980s in the aftermath of the gasoline price shocks of the 1970s. Those studies found that higher gasoline prices increased the demand for smaller, morefuel-efficient vehicles relative to larger, less-efficient vehicles.[3] That relationship continues to hold with recent vehicle sales, according to several current economic studies.[4]

MARKET SHARES FOR CARS AND LIGHT TRUCKS

Sales of new cars as a share of all passenger vehicle sales increased noticeably in late 2005. Through August of that year, the share of cars was unchanged from its year- to-date share in August 2004. But light-truck sales in autumn 2005 were weaker than usual as businesses and consumers first experienced gasoline prices in excess of $3 per gallon after Hurricane Katrina.[5] For the full year of 2005, cars constituted 45 percent of new-vehicle sales, almost a full percentage point higher than in 2004. The share since then has been even higher, around 47 percent (see Figure 2-1).

The upturn in the market share of cars since 2004 is particularly noteworthy because that share had been in decline for 25 years, falling lower every year after 1981, when more than 80 percent of new passenger vehicles were cars. The decline reflects the increasing popularity of minivans and, later, of SUVs and crossover vehicles, and the declining popularity of some types of cars, particularly station wagons. The adoption of corporate average fuel economy regulations contributed to that shift by requiring higher average fuel economy for cars than for light trucks, which led to the development of the minivan, a light-truck alternative to the station wagon. Because most minivans had relatively good fuel economy compared with that of other light trucks, and most station wagons had relatively poor fuel economy compared with that of other cars, the shift in the demand for high- capacity passenger vehicles from station wagons toward the more popular minivan helped automakers satisfy CAFE standards both for cars and for light trucks.[6]

Between 2004 and 2006, every major category of car gained and every category of light truck lost market share (see Table 2-1). The biggest gain was for large cars, which went from 8.0 percent to 9.4 percent of the market. The share of midsize cars also increased considerably, and although the market shares of compact and subcompact cars also increased, those gains were smaller. The underlying sales data indicate that those gains in market share for the most part reflect a decline in sales of light trucks (in every category) rather than an increase in car sales. Overall, the number of cars sold actually declined by about 1.5 percent each year from 2004 to 2006, or by a little more than 100,000 cars per year. (Sales in the large-car category increased by 10 percent.) However, over that same period, sales of light trucks fell by 10 percent, with nearly 1 million fewer new vehicles sold per year. (For 2007, August year-to-date unit sales of light trucks were down an additional 2 percent compared with the same period in 2006. However, car sales were 4 percent lower.)

Table 2-1. Market Shares of Different Types of New Vehicles, 2004 to 2006

(Percent)				Change 2004 to 2006	
	2004	2005	2006	Absolute (Percentage points)	Percentage Change
Cars					
Subcompact and two-seater	1.3	1.3	1.4	0.1	3.8
Compact	19.2	19.8	19.4	0.2	0.8
Midsize	16.3	16.4	17.0	0.7	4.3
Large	8.0	8.5	9.4	1.4	14.4
Calendar Year Sales (Millions of vehicles)	7.6	7.8	7.5		
Change from Previous Year (Percent)	-1.2	2.2	-3.6		
Light Trucks					
Minivan	6.3	6.4	6.0	-0.3	-4.4
SUV	27.2	26.6	26.8	-0.4	-1.3
Pickup truck	18.4	18.6	17.8	-0.6	-3.3
Passenger or cargo van	3.3	2.3	2.2	-1.1	-32.0
Calendar Year Sales (Millions of vehicles)	9.4	9.1	8.4		
Change from Previous Year (Percent)	6.0	-3.3	-7.8		

Source: Congressional Budget Office based on data published in *Automotive News*.
Notes: SUV = sport–utility vehicle.

    Market shares total 100 percent.

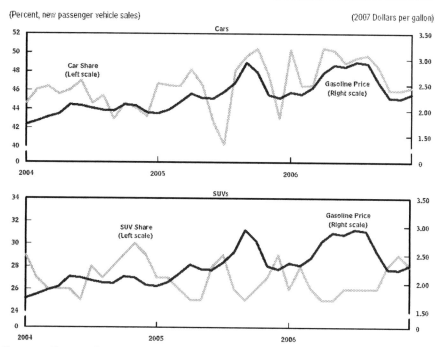

Sources: Congressional Budget Office based on data from *Automotive News* and the Department of Energy, Energy Information Administration.

Note: The right-hand scale shows the average inflation-adjusted price per gallon for all grades and formulations of gasoline.

Figure 2-2. Passenger Vehicle Market Shares and the Real Price of Gasoline, 2004 to 2006.

Despite the relatively large decline in light-truck sales, the data do not indicate the extent to which the increase in market share for cars occurred because would-be truck buyers merely delayed their truck purchases versus buying a car instead. The small decline in sales of cars could even be consistent with a large number of would-be truck buyers switching to cars and averting what might otherwise have been a larger decline in car sales. Such a possibility also is consistent with the considerable gains that occurred for large-car sales, because among all car types, large cars are the closest substitute for light trucks in terms of seating, storage capacity, and engine size. To the extent that some truck buyers have delayed purchasing a truck rather than switching to a car, sustained high gasoline prices could eventually lead to more car sales because consumers must eventually replace their existing vehicles.

GASOLINE PRICES AND VEHICLE MARKET SHARES

A comparison of monthly data on the market shares of different types of vehicles against monthly average retail gasoline prices suggests that some light-truck buyers may have briefly delayed purchasing a new truck while gasoline prices were increasing. Price spikes in the spring of 2005, in October 2005 (after Hurricane Katrina), and in the spring of 2006 all coincided with sharp increases in the new-car market share (see Figure 2-2). Market shares for leading categories of light trucks—especially SUVs— went the opposite way, dipping as gasoline prices rose. When the price of gasoline has dropped, the market share of each vehicle type has tended to return to previous levels. Some of those movements in market share could be influenced by manufacturers' sales incentives, which vary from one month to the next and sometimes are relatively stronger for cars, sometimes for light trucks. However, exploratory analysis of recent data on incentives, described later, suggests the incentives account for little of the variation in the relative market shares of cars and light trucks.

To assess the degree to which gasoline prices and vehicle market shares are related statistically, the Congressional Budget Office analyzed 36 months of data from January 2004 through December 2006 on sales of each type of vehicle. CBO computed the market shares from monthly sales data for specific vehicle models (for example, Toyota Camry), aggregated into total sales by vehicle category (for example, midsize cars). The aggregations are based on vehicle classifications from the fuel economy ratings published by the Environmental Protection Agency (EPA).

BOX 2-1. MODELING THE INFLUENCE OF THE PRICE OF GASOLINE ON VEHICLE MARKET SHARES

The gasoline price that the Congressional Budget Office (CBO) used in its analysis is the U.S. average monthly retail price for all grades and formulations. CBO's statistical model consists of a system of equations, one for each vehicle category (the sum of all of the market shares is necessarily 100 percent, so one vehicle category must be excluded to prevent the system of equations from being linearly dependent and thus inestimable). It is estimated as a "seemingly unrelated regression" model:

$$[\text{vehicle category market share}]_j =$$

$$\alpha_j + \beta_{1j} \times (\text{real gasoline price}) +$$

$$\beta_{2j} \times (\text{winter}) + \beta_{3j} \times (\text{spring}) +$$

$$\beta_{4j} \times (\text{summer}) + \varepsilon_j$$

where j is a type of vehicle (subcompact, compact, midsize, large, minivan, sport–utility vehicle, or pickup; the omitted category is cargo– passenger van). The β_{1j} terms represent percentage-point changes in market share that are attributable to changes in gasoline prices. As a check, CBO also estimated each equation separately, with an autoregressive error term ε of degree 1 (to account for the tendency for market shares to remain above or below their long-term averages for more than a month at a time). Each approach yielded similar results.

Current gasoline prices and the market shares of specific types of vehicles should be related to the extent that current prices influence consumers' expectations about future prices and to the extent that vehicle operating costs (primarily fuel costs) influence consumers' decisions about which vehicles to purchase.[7] CBO's analysis of the relationship between gasoline prices and vehicle market shares accounts for seasonal effects, a possible source of correlation between market shares and gasoline prices if both exhibit seasonal variation.[8]

On the basis of that reasoning, CBO constructed a model in which the market shares of different vehicle types are influenced by the current average inflation-adjusted price of gasoline and the current season (see Box 2-1).[9] According to the model, the effect of gasoline prices on U.S. new-vehicle market shares has been such that a price increase of 60 cents per gallon (a 20 percent increase if the base price is $3 per gallon) is associated with an aver-age increase in the market share of new cars of 2.6 percentage points (the sample average is 46.4 percent). That result reflects recent experience, although consumers' future responses also would be affected by changes in automakers' product offerings and pricing (which are also responsive to rising gasoline prices).

All major car categories—from two-seaters and subcompacts to large sedans and wagons—have gained market share as the price of gasoline has risen, with gains of between 4.5 percent and about 9 percent for every 60 cent increase in the price of gasoline above $2.30 per gallon. At the same time, the market shares of all types of light trucks, from minivans and SUVs to pickup trucks and passenger or cargo vans, have fallen by 4 percent to 6 percent. For example, at average values, a 60 cent increase in the price of gasoline would have increased the market share of midsize cars by about 0.8 percentage points, which is a 5 percent increase over its average value of 16.6 percent. That price increase also would be associated with a decline of 1.2 percentage points or 4.5 percent in the share of new SUVs, on average, from a baseline share of about 27 percent (see Table 2-2).

Table 2-2. Estimated Effect of a 20 Percent Increase in the Price of Gasoline on U.S. Market Shares of New Passenger Vehicles

(Percent)				
	Average Market Share[a]	**Average Effect of Increase (Percentage points)**[b]	**Statistical Significance**	**Relative Change In Market Share**[c]
Cars (Versus light trucks)	46.4	+2.6	**	+5.6
Cars				
Subcompact or two-seater	1.4	+0.1	*	+6.8
Compact	19.7	+0.9	*	+4.5
Midsize	16.6	+0.8	*	+5.0
Large	8.7	+0.8	**	+9.4
Light Trucks				
Minivan	6.2	-0.3	*	-5.0
SUV	26.9	-1.2	**	-4.5
Pickup truck	18.2	-1.0	*	-5.7
Passenger or cargo van	2.3	-0.1	b	-3.9
Total Cars and Light Trucks	**100**	**0**	n.a	n.a.

Source: Congressional Budget Office based on vehicle sales data from *Automotive News* and gasoline price data from the Department of Energy, Energy Information Administration.

Note: ** = significant at 1 percent; * = significant at 5 percent; SUV = sport–utility vehicle; n.a. = not applicable.

a. Market share averages are not sales weighted.

b. Over all vehicle categories, the net change in market share must be zero. Thus, a value of -0.1 for the market share of "passenger or cargo van" is not estimated directly but is derived from changes in the market shares of other vehicles.

c. Percentage increase in market share given in first column when percentage points in second column are added to it.

The results in Table 2-2 might not reflect the full shift in demand toward greater fuel economy, because automobile manufacturers can respond to higher gasoline prices—and to slower sales of light trucks—by offering incentives to purchasers to reduce inventories of new vehicles. CBO examined data on finance rate and price incentives for February 2006 through October 2006 and found that, during the summer of 2006, when gasoline prices were above $3 per gallon, the average financing rates that automakers were offering on some models of light truck did decline somewhat relative to the rates offered on some cars. (Incentives were not offered on all models every month, and for some models, no incentives were offered in any month.) Some consumers thus might have been encouraged to purchase a light truck when they otherwise would have chosen a car, partially counteracting the effect of higher gasoline prices on consumers' decisions about which new vehicle to purchase and leading to slightly smaller gasoline price effects.

CHANGES IN NEW-VEHICLE FUEL ECONOMY AND PRICING

The 2005 model year might have marked a turning point not only in the long, steady decline in the new-car market share but also in the declining average fuel economy of new passenger vehicles. The recent increase in market share for new cars is responsible for some of the increase in the average fuel economy for the vehicle fleet; on average, a car can travel about 6.5 miles farther on a gallon of gasoline than a light truck can, according to data from EPA (see Figure 2-3).

However, the average fuel economy of new cars has itself been rising. Beginning with the 2001 model year, when the average fuel economy rating for new cars was 28.4 miles per gallon, the average began to increase, peaking at 29.2 mpg for the 2005 model year before slipping back slightly in 2006.[10] Another reason for the increase in average new-vehicle fuel economy is that since 2005, automobile manufacturers have had to meet stricter CAFE standards for light trucks. An increasingly popular new kind of light truck, often called a crossover vehicle because it is built on a car chassis but with the higher clearance of a light truck (and thus is so classified for CAFE purposes), also is partly responsible for the rise in the average fuel economy of light trucks and may reflect, in part, a response by automakers to higher CAFE standards for light trucks. The CAFE standard for cars did not change. (Legislation

signed in December 2007 requires a substantial increase in the average fuel
economy of all new passenger vehicles sold in the United States. By 2020, the
CAFE standard will increase to 35 mpg.[11])

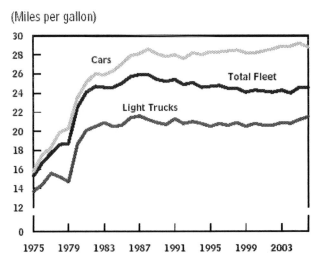

Sources: Congressional   Budget   Office   based   on   data   from   the
            Environmental Protection Agency (EPA).

Note: Data are for sales-weighted fuel economy. Although a vehicle's fuel economy
      performance is determined by EPA, either through EPA's laboratory results or in
      test data submitted by the manufacturer, it is the National Highway Traffic Safety
      Administration (NHTSA) that determines compliance with corporate average fuel
      economy (CAFE) standards. NHTSA considers CAFE credits the automaker has
      earned, including those for hybrid and dual-fuel vehicles. NHTSA's CAFE data
      are similar to those illustrated here, although the averages are slightly higher
      because of the credits.

Figure 2-3. Average Rated Fuel Economy for New U.S. Passenger Vehicles, 1975 to
2006.

Although the average fuel economy ratings of cars and light trucks alike
have been increasing since 2002, the average fuel economy for all new
passenger vehicles declined through 2004 because the market share for light
trucks was still rising at that time. Higher gasoline prices cannot explain why
average new-car fuel economy ratings began to increase in 2001, because
gasoline prices did not start rising until 2003 (see Table 2-3). However,
gasoline prices have risen steadily since then, helping to increase the demand
for vehicles that are more fuel efficient.

Table 2-3. National Average Gasoline Prices, 2000 to 2006

(Dollars per gallon)		
	Average Price	
	Nominal	**2007 Dollars**
2000	1.52	1.82
2001	1.47	1.70
2002	1.38	1.58
2003	1.60	1.79
2004	1.89	2.06
2005	2.31	2.43
2006	2.62	2.66

Source: Congressional Budget Office based on data from the Department of Energy, Energy Information Administration (for nominal prices) and from the Department of Commerce, Bureau of Labor Statistics (real prices calcluated from the consumer product index for all urban consumers).

Note: Prices are for all grades and all formulations

That increased demand and the resulting improvement in vehicle fuel economy appear to have affected the pricing of some new vehicles. In the past, some automakers might have set lower prices on fuel-efficient vehicles— and higher prices on other vehicles—as part of their overall strategy to meet CAFE standards; an increase in demand for fuel-efficient vehicles would permit automakers to rely less on pricing to meet the standards. If so, prices of new fuel-efficient vehicles should have increased relative to prices of larger, less-efficient vehicles. There is some evidence that that has occurred (see Box 2-2), meaning that the rise in average fuel economy for new vehicles does not fully reflect the shift in consumer preferences toward greater fuel efficiency.

CHANGES IN THE USED-VEHICLE MARKET

The recently observed price shifts for new vehicles are reflected in used-vehicle prices as well. Average prices of fuel-efficient used vehicles have been rising, and those of less-efficient vehicles have been falling. That is as expected: In both markets, consumers' preferences for fuel-efficient vehicles should be similarly affected by rising gasoline prices—which should affect prices similarly in both markets. Even if consumers' preferences were not affected in exactly the same way by gasoline prices, price increases on fuel-efficient new vehicles would cause the prices on similar used vehicles to rise as some consumers shifted from buying new vehicles to buying similar used vehicles. Similarly, smaller price increases on less-fuelefficient new vehicles would limit how quickly prices could rise for comparable used vehicles. New-vehicle prices serve as a ceiling on consumers' willingness to pay for used (noncollectible) vehicles.[12]

Consistent with a shift in consumer demand toward greater fuel economy, monthly average prices in the United States for used vehicles in the large-SUV and luxury car categories declined steadily over the 49 months for which CBO collected data, through July 2006. Over the same period, average prices increased for sporty, full- size, and compact or midsize used cars (see Table 2-4).[13] It is not possible to attribute those price changes definitively to vehicles' fuel economy ratings, because the data do not include information on other characteristics (such as the age of the vehicles or prices when new) that also could have contributed to the price trends. However, those trends are consistent with the new-vehicle market: Prices for small vehicles have been rising while those for larger vehicles have fallen or, for new cars, have risen more slowly (see Figure 2-4).

Table 2-4. Average Monthly Change in Price of Used Vehicles, 2002 to 2006

	Monthly Mean Price Change (Percent)	Average Change (Dollars)	Statistical Significance
Full-Size Car	0.58	47	***
Sporty Car	0.54	64	***
Compact or Midsize Car	0.47	33	***
Minivan	0.15	12	**
Small Pickup Truck	0.12	8	*
"Other" SUV[a]	0.01	2	n.s.
Full-Size Pickup Truck	-0.04	-5	n.s.
Small or Midsize SUV	-0.07	-7	*
Luxury Car	-0.20	-28	***
Large SUV	-0.49	-72	***

Source: Congressional Budget Office based on monthly average used-vehicle prices and vehicle classifications from *Automotive News*.

Note: *** = significant at <0.01 percent; ** = significant at <5 percent; * = significant at <10 percent; n.s. = not significant at conventional levels; SUV = sport–utility vehicle.

Figure 2-4 displays average prices for the vehicle categories with the strongest and most statistically significant price trends. Although the data do not include information about the average size or weight of vehicles in each category, the category names are an indication of likely differences in vehicle size. Based on category names alone, the price trends in Figure 2-4 suggest that vehicles with declining prices are larger than average and thus are likely to have fuel economy ratings below the applicable CAFE standard. The vehicle categories with increasing prices seem likely to include somewhat smaller-thanaverage vehicles with higher fuel economy ratings. (Compliance with CAFE standards is determined on the basis of an automaker's fleetwide average fuel economy, so vehicles with ratings lower than the applicable standard do not subject the automaker to penalties if they are balanced by sales of more-fuel-efficient vehicles.) The average monthly dollar changes in vehicle prices corresponding to the sloping trend lines in Figure 2-4 are given in Table 2-4.

a. Includes SUVs, luxury sport wagons, and small sport wagons.

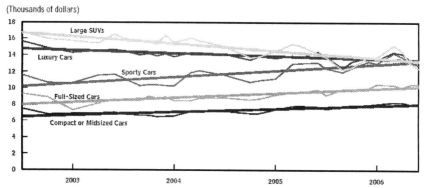

Source: Congressional Budget Office based on data published in *Automotive News*.
Notes: SUV = sport–utility vehicle.
Automobile category names are from *Automotive News*. Data are monthly sales figures. Straight lines are trend lines added by CBO.

Figure 2-4. Average Wholesale Prices for Used Vehicles, July 2002 to July 2006.

BOX 2-2. CAFE IMPLICATIONS OF RISING AVERAGE FUEL ECONOMY

For the 2006 model year, list prices of new vehicles with higher fuel economy ratings rose more quickly, in relation to 2005 list prices, than did prices of other new vehicles. For models sold in both years, there is a positive correlation, which is statistically significant at the 1 percent level, between a model's fuel economy rating (in either year) and the percentage increase in its MSRP, the manufacturer's suggested retail price.[1] That correlation implies that a fuel economy difference of one mile per gallon between any two car models is associated with a 0.24 percentage-point bigger price increase for the car that is more fuel efficient. That difference is considerable, given that the average price increase for new cars was 1.2 percent for 2006 models (see the table on the facing page). Similar, if slightly weaker, relationships exist for SUVs (sport–utility vehicles) and for minivans. (The correlations for SUVs and minivans are just as large but are statistically weaker because they are based on fewer models.)

Automakers that achieve higher average fuel economy ratings have more latitude in maintaining compliance with corporate average fuel economy (CAFE) standards. By contrast, companies that just meet the standards might not be able to raise prices for their more-fuel-efficient vehicles as much as they otherwise would, for example, because their CAFE ratings would fall if the higher prices caused too many purchasers to choose other vehicles instead.

To see whether vehicle list prices are consistent with the notion that automakers constrained by CAFE standards have less latitude in setting prices, the Congressional Budget Office compared the MSRPs from four manufacturers for the 2005 and 2006 model years. Two of the companies, Ford and General Motors (GM), had relatively little latitude in maintaining compliance with one or both types of CAFE standard (for cars and for light trucks). Honda and Toyota, by contrast, had CAFE ratings well above the standards in both years. The differences in CAFE compliance margins were reflected in all four automakers' list prices for the 2005 and 2006 model years.

The prices Ford and GM set for their 2006 cars, relative to the 2005 prices for the same models, were significantly and negatively correlated with the cars' fuel economy ratings. That is, Ford and GM raised prices *less* for models that got better gas mileage than they did for their other models. Honda and Toyota raised prices *more* for their more-fuel-efficient cars. The price increases for Honda and Toyota light trucks followed a similar pattern. The changes from 2005 to 2006 in the list prices of Ford and GM light trucks showed no statistical correlation with the fuel economy ratings of those vehicles.

Given the increased demand for fuel-efficient vehicles, that difference in pricing strategies is consistent with the CAFE standards' having induced Ford and GM to sell larger numbers of fuel-efficient vehicles than they otherwise would. However, the longer gasoline prices stay above their historic levels, and the greater the shift in consumers' preferences toward improved fuel efficiency, the easier it will become for automakers to comply with the current standards.

[1] The Congressional Budget Office (CBO) adjusted the year-to-year price changes for differences in standard equipment, using equipment and vehicle price data from the 2005 and 2006 editions of the *Automotive News Market Data Book.* The MSRP is not the same as the actual transaction price, which will include any manufacturers' incentives and is the result of negotiation between the dealer and the customer. CBO does not have transaction prices.

Average Change in MSRP, 2005 to 2006, for Models Sold Both Years

	Number of Models Compared	Average Change in MSRP, 2005 to 2006[a] (Percent)	Correlation (Change in MSRP and fuel economy)	Statistical Significance (*p* value)
Car	104	1.2	0.24	0.013
Minivan	16	0.3	0.54	0.032
SUV	63	0.3	0.25	0.044
Pickup Truck	13	-2.3	0.08	0.795
Overall	196	0.2[b]	0.33	<0.0001

Source: Congressional Budget Office based on data from *Automotive News.*

Notes: MSRP = manufacturer's suggested retail price; *p* = probability; SUV = sport–utility vehicle. Analysis based on 2005 fuel economy ratings yields similar results.

a. Nominal prices for identical models, adjusted for differences in standard equipment. Nominal prices are used because there was little change in the consumer price index for automobiles from 2005 to 2006. Averages weighted by August 2006 year-to-date sales.

b. Not a measure of average price increase for all vehicles, only for those included in this analysis.

End Notes

1 For a concise introduction to corporate average fuel economy standards, see Congressional Budget Office, *The Economic Costs of Fuel Economy Standards Versus a Gasoline Tax* (December 2003), p.2.

2 See Congressional Budget Office, *Budget Options* (February 2005), Option 32, p. 308. The phaseout was mandated by the American Jobs Creation Act of 2004.

3 John Greenlees discussed the effects on new-vehicle demand in "Gasoline Prices and Purchases of New Automobiles," *Southern Economic Journal,* vol. 47, no. 1 (1980), pp. 167–178. For evidence that used-vehicle demand responds similarly to gasoline prices, see George G. Daly and Thomas H. Mayor, "Reason and Rationality During Energy Crises," *Journal of Political Economy,* vol. 19, no. 1 (1983), pp. 168–181; and James Kahn, "Gasoline Prices and the Used Automobile Market: A Rational Expectations Asset Price Approach," *Quarterly Journal of Economics,* vol. 101, no. 2 (1986), pp. 323–340.

4 See, for example, Joshua Linn and Thomas Klier, "Gasoline Prices and the Demand for New Vehicles: Evidence from Monthly Sales Data" (working paper, March 2007), http://tigger.uic.edu/~jlinn/ vehicles.pdf; and Sarah West, "The Effect of Gasoline Prices on the Demand for Sport Utility Vehicles," (prepared for a session on "Demand Estimation in Environmental Economics," Midwest Economics Association Meetings, March 2007), www.macalester.edu/~wests/SarahWestMEA2007.pdf. For a more general treatment, see Walter McManus, "The Link Between Gasoline Prices and Vehicle Sales: Economic Theory Trumps Conventional Detroit Wisdom," *Business Economics (*January 2007), pp. 53–60.

5 According to data published in *Automotive News,* a trade publication, in other recent years, the share of light-truck sales was *higher* in the autumn than in the rest of the year. For 2003, 2004, and 2006, the August year-to-date market share for light trucks was 1 to 2 percentage points lower than the full-year share, indicating stronger light-truck sales for September through December.

6 See Congressional Budget Office, *The Economic Costs of Fuel Economy Standards Versus a Gasoline Tax.* Automakers' CAFE ratings depend not only on the mix of vehicles they sell but also on the fuel economy rating of each model. As automotive technologies have become more fuel efficient, automakers have been able either to improve fuel economy or to add fuel-consuming features (such as more horsepower) without reducing fuel economy. With lower gasoline prices, consumers tended to favor other attributes over fuel economy, and many manufacturers' CAFE ratings stayed flat, despite technological advances. Higher gasoline prices have led to a shift in consumer preferences toward greater fuel economy.

7 Current gasoline prices could reflect consumers' best forecast of likely future prices—what economists call "static" expectations. (For empirical evidence, see Daly and Mayor, "Reason and Rationality During Energy Crises," an examination of vehicle prices in the wake of the 1973 and 1979 oil price increases.) Consumers also could implicitly make more sophisticated, "dynamic" price projections by, in effect, averaging prices observed in recent months. It is straightforward to model such expectations, but it is not considered here. Given the recent upward trend in gasoline prices and the downward trend in the market share for light trucks, such a model would probably yield results similar to those of the static model.

8 Gasoline prices typically rise in the warmer months as longer daylight hours and vacation travel increase demand. Light-truck sales recently have tended to be higher in the autumn, when gasoline prices usually are below their annual peak.

9 A more thorough analysis would incorporate the effects of relative vehicle prices. Automakers have responded to rising gasoline prices by raising the prices of smaller vehicles relative to those for larger ones. Thus, CBO's analysis could understate the effects of gasoline prices

on the market share of a given type of vehicle, because some of those effects would have been partly neutralized by changing vehicle prices.

[10] From 2003 to 2006, midsize cars made the biggest gain in sales- weighted average fuel economy, increasing from 23.9 mpg to 25.3 mpg. Among light trucks, the biggest increase was for SUVs, which went from 18.3 mpg in 2003 to 19.5 mpg in 2006. Sizable improvements also were made by compact cars and minivans. The averages reflect EPA's adjustment of about 15 percent below the vehicles' CAFE ratings to account for estimated differences between laboratory-measured and actual fuel economy. EPA will begin using a new method of adjustment in 2008. See Robert M. Heavenrich, *Light-Duty Automotive Technology and Fuel Economy Trends: 1975 Through 2006,* EPA420-R-06-01 1 (Environmental Protection Agency, Office of Transportation and Air Quality, Advanced Technology Division, July 2006), p. A-10, *www.epa.gov/otaq/cert/mpg/ fetrends/420r06011.pdf;* and Environmental Protection Agency, Office of Transportation and Air Quality, Compliance and Innovative Strategies Division and Transportation Compliance Division, *Light-Duty Automotive Technology and Fuel Economy Trends: 1975 Through 2007,* EPA420-R-07-008 (September 2007), p. A-9, www.epa.gov/otaq/ cert/mpg/fetrends/420r07008a.pdf.

[11] See the Energy Independence and Security Act of 2007. For model years 1996 to 2004, the CAFE standard for light trucks was 20.7 mpg. It was raised to 21 mpg for 2005 and 21.6 mpg for 2006. The standard is now 22.2 mpg for light trucks in model years 2007 and later. The CAFE standard for cars, unchanged since 1990, is 27.5 mpg. See National Highway Traffic Safety Administration, "CAFE Overview, Frequently Asked Questions," www.nhtsa.dot.gov/cars/rules/cafe/overview.htm.

[12] Although CAFE standards apply only to new vehicles, they also can affect prices of used vehicles: Where some manufacturers' pricing is affected by the standards, as when just-compliant manufacturers offer lower prices on their fuel-efficient vehicles to boost sales and CAFE ratings, those lower prices will attract some potential buyers of used vehicles, thus reducing the demand for (and average prices of) fuel-efficient used vehicles.

[13] The used-vehicle classifications are from *Automotive News.*

In: Gasoline Prices and their Effects on Behavior   ISBN: 978-1-60741-351-6
Editor: Hermann Schreiber   © 2010 Nova Science Publishers, Inc.

Chapter 3

APPENDIX A. STUDY DATA

Congressional Budget Office

The Congressional Budget Office (CBO) constructed the highway traffic data set for this study from data gathered through an extensive network of electronic sensors embedded in urban and suburban highway travel lanes throughout the state of California.[1] The available data describe traffic flow (vehicle counts), lane occupancy rates, and vehicle speeds in every lane at thousands of locations. In the sample that CBO constructed from those data, sensor readings date back at least to 2003, and for many locations, they begin several years earlier. The data can be assembled for periods of as little as five minutes or for much longer intervals. In this study, CBO analyzed 24-hour vehicle totals for Wednesdays, Saturdays, and Sundays, and the distribution of speeds observed over an entire month, on Saturdays and Sundays only, by hour of the day.

CBO collected data on total vehicle flows at 13 representative locations around California; speed data were gathered from 3 of those locations. The locations were chosen to represent traffic conditions in all of California's major metropolitan areas. They were not chosen randomly, but the data were not inspected before inclusion in the sample.[2]

The locations selected represent areas of moderate to relatively high (for California) population density. They include locations that are adjacent to rail transit systems as well as those with no nearby rail option. The data exclude locations with the potential for localized congestion, as from lane reduction bottlenecks or merges ahead. The sample includes interstate, U.S., and state highways. Most locations have four lanes in each direction; two locations have three lanes, and two have five lanes. Except where noted, measurements were made on inbound lanes only, where the direction of travel is toward city centers (see Table A-1 on page 28).

TOTAL TRIPS

CBO collected traffic volume data for Wednesdays, Saturdays, and Sundays through the end of 2006. The sample includes data for Saturdays and Sundays because their typical traffic volumes differ considerably. In CBO's highway sample, there is about 10 percent less highway travel on Saturdays and 20 percent less on Sundays than on a typical weekday. Wednesday totals are representative of weekday traffic, with Wednesdays least affected by three-day weekend travel. CBO's sample excludes other weekdays to avoid needlessly introducing holiday-related variation into the data. In urban areas and outlying suburbs, highway travel demand tends to be relatively high on Fridays and Mondays around three-day holiday weekends and lower on the weekends. Travel also varies seasonally (it is typically highest in summer, lowest in winter). CBO's analysis accounts for all of those effects on highway travel.

Figure A-1 shows daily vehicle flows since 1999 in the westbound lanes of I-8 in San Diego. The data show traffic rising to a peak of about 100,000 vehicles per weekday in mid-2002 and then gently declining through 2005. That could have been caused by shifts in regional development patterns and in economic conditions at that location. CBO accounts for such influences by including a trend line for each of the 13 locations in the analysis and allowing those lines to curve upward or downward as dictated by the data.[3]

The analysis also accounts for other factors that could explain differences in volume at different locations and on different days. Many potential factors, such as number of lanes, population density, or proximity to employment centers, are accounted for by including a fixed factor for each location–day. Including those factors in the model allows the effect of gasoline prices on traffic volume to be estimated independently of other factors that also affect the demand for passenger vehicle travel.

The several unusual one-day drops or increases in the figure mostly indicate holidays. The extended drop in late 2005 was caused by a detector outage of several weeks. The outliers are included in the analysis, but are attributed to holidays or the effects of offline detectors (thus, not to gasoline prices) as appropriate.

The analysis expresses traffic volume as a percentage of the average baseline volume (from a period before the study began) at each location. That accounts for the likelihood that a change in weekly average gasoline prices will have a similar percentage effect on daily traffic volumes that week at locations with different amounts of traffic, as opposed to affecting similar numbers of trips at locations carrying different numbers of vehicles. Gasoline prices also are expressed in relative terms, as a percentage change from a baseline price, to allow a given percentage price change to have a consistent effect on traffic volumes at different times.

CBO's analysis assumes that gasoline prices are independent of local demand for highway travel. Changes in the price of gasoline are determined largely by changes in global supplies of and demand for oil and in the cost of refining that oil into gasoline. In recent years, the price of gasoline in U.S. markets has been substantially influenced by growth in the demand for oil in countries with rapidly developing economies, such as China.[4] Regional constraints on supplies can cause gasoline prices to be higher in some areas than in others, but within California, supply constraints do not differ substantially.

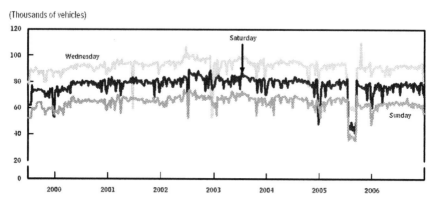

Source: Congressional Budget Office based on data from the Freeway Performance Measurement Project, https://pems.eecs.berkeley.edu.

Note: Daily traffic recorded on westbound Interstate 8, Lake Murray Boulevard, San Diego, California.

Figure A-1. Daily Traffic Volume, I-8, San Diego, California.

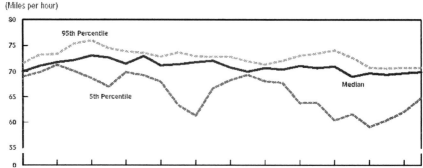

Source: Congressional Budget Office based on data from the Freeway Performance
    Measurement Project, https://pems.eecs.berkeley.edu.
Note: Data come from sensors located on northbound Interstate 680 at Montevideo
    Drive, San Ramon (in East Bay, San Francisco).

Figure A-2. Weekend Speeds on I-680, San Ramon, California, April 2006.

VEHICLE SPEED

CBO analyzed four years of monthly average gasoline prices against the
same months' characteristic vehicle speeds at different locations and times of
day. Figure A-2 provides an example, showing vehicle speed data for April
2006 for a northbound section of Interstate 680 near Montevideo Drive in San
Ramon, California—one of the three sampled locations. For each location,
CBO collected vehicle speed data from January 2003 through December 2006.
Figure A-2 shows the median, 5th percentile, and 95th percentile speeds
observed at each hour of the day on Saturdays and Sundays in April 2006.

The figure indicates, for example, that between 2 p.m. and 3 p.m., the 5th
percentile weekend speed was 68.1 miles per hour (mph). The median speed
was 70.7 mph. The 95th percentile speed was 71.4 mph. Tests of hypotheses
that drivers react differently to gasoline prices according to their value of time
actually are tests for whether prices affect speeds more at the slow end of the
distribution than at the median or at the faster end. Support for that
interpretation is given with the results.[5]

Sometimes there is mild traffic congestion on weekends. Figure A-1
shows that speeds peak in the predawn hours and gradually decline through 2
p.m. Another peak occurs at 6 p.m. Other months and other locations exhibit
slightly different patterns. The 5th percentile speeds in Figure A-2 provide

stronger evidence for congestion: They are as much as 10 mph slower than the median speeds. That pattern could be due to a one-time slowdown (as from an accident, road work, poor weather, special event, or simply a random surge in traffic), or it could originate in recurring congestion that affects only a fraction of vehicles.[6]

Table A-1.Vehicle Detector Stations in Sample

Route (Direction)	Location	Comments	Type of Data	Rail Option?
		Sacramento		
I-80 (E)[a]	Mace Boulevard, Davis	Eastern edge of Davis, 9 miles west of Sacramento	Trips	No
CA 99 (N)	47th Avenue, Sacramento	Adjacent, parallel to Sacramento RT (light rail) 4 miles from city center	Trips	Yes
US 50 (W)	Folsom Boulevard and La Riviera Drive, Sacramento	Adjacent, parallel to Sacramento RT (light rail) 6 miles from city center	Trips	Yes
		San Francisco Bay Area		
I-680 (N)	Montevideo Drive, San Ramon (San Ramon Valley)	Lateral route (neither inbound nor outbound)	Trips, Speed	No
CA 24 (W)	El Nido Ranch Road, Lafayette	Adjacent, parallel to BART (heavy rail) 7 miles east of Oakland, 11 miles east of San Francisco	Trips	Yes
I-880 (N)	98th Avenue, San Leandro	Adjacent, parallel to BART (heavy rail) 7 miles south of Oakland, 11 miles from San Francisco	Trips	Yes
CA 101 (N)	Poplar and Peninsula Avenues, San Mateo	Parallel to CalTrain (commuter train) 17 miles south of San Francisco (downtown)	Trips	No[b]
		Los Angeles and Orange County		
CA 101 (S)	Barham Boulevard, Universal City and Hollywood	Adjacent, parallel to L.A. Metro Red Line (heavy rail) 9miles northwest of downtown Los Angeles	Trips	Yes
I-105 (W)	South Central Avenue, South-Central Los Angeles	Adjacent, parallel to L.A. Metro Green Line (light rail) 11 miles south of downtown Los Angeles	Trips	Yes
I-405 (S)	Newland Street, Westminster (Orange County)	Outbound for Long Beach and Los Angeles but inbound for Orange County (Costa Mesa, Irvine, and Newport	Trips, Speed	No

Table A-1. (Continued)

Route (Direction)	Location	Comments	Type of Data	Rail Option?
		Beach). High-occupancy-vehicle lane not analyzed.		
		San Diego County		
I-15 (N)	Scripps Poway Parkway, Poway (North San Diego County)	Outbound direction, 10 miles north of San Diego[c]	Trips	No
I-5 (S)	Lomas Santa Fe Drive, Solana Beach (North San Diego County)	Parallel to NCTD Coaster (commuter train), 17 miles north of San Diego (downtown)	Trips	No[b]
I-8 (W)	Lake Murray Boulevard, San Diego	Adjacent, parallel to San Diego Trolley (light rail), 7miles east of San Diego (downtown)	Trips, Speed	Yes

Source: Congressional Budget Office.

Notes: I= Interstate; CA = California state route; US = U.S. route; E = east; N = north; W = west; S = south; NCTD = North County (San Diego) Transit District; RT = rapid transit; BART = Bay Area Rapid Transit; LA = Los Angeles.

According to statistics published by the American Public Transportation Association (www.apta.com), in the third quarter of 2006, average weekday ridership totals for the transit systems were as follows: BART (heavy rail), 355,400; LA Metro (light rail), 129,000; LA Metro (heavy rail), 125,900; San Diego Trolley (light rail), 107,300; Sacramento Regional Transit (light rail), 54,400; CalTrain (commuter train), 36,200; NCTD (commuter train), 6,300. Those figures are not directly comparable because of differences in track miles, but on the basis of passengers per mile of track, ridership on the two commuter train systems is relatively low: LA Metro (heavy rail), 3,690; BART, 1,330; LA Metro (light rail), 1,110; San Diego Trolley, 1,110; Sacramento Regional Transit, 870; CalTrain, 260; NCTD, 80. Because the freeways adjacent to the two train systems (CalTrain and NCTD) carry about as much traffic as the other freeways in the sample, those figures imply that the two train systems carry a much lower fraction of commuters in those locations compared with the light- and heavy-rail systems.

a. Carries substantial Sierra-bound weekend recreation traffic; reported results exclude that route.

b. CBO analysis treats routes served by commuter train as "no transit" routes: Ridership is lower than on light- and heavy-rail systems because of lower capacity and less frequent service.

c. Inbound I-15 (S) has a notorious traffic bottleneck.

CBO's analysis accounts for the effects of congestion so that they do not influence the estimated effect of gasoline prices on speeds. The analysis accounts for slowdowns caused by relatively severe congestion and for differences in traffic volume from one month to the next.[7] It also accounts for congestion that is related to the time of day by incorporating fixed factors for location and hour into the statistical model. (Those factors also account for differences by location in speed limits and in the physical characteristics of the roadway, such as grade, curvature, distance from ramps, number and width of lanes, and type and condition of pavement.[8]) Time-of-day variation in traffic speed cannot be attributed to fluctuating gasoline prices, because prices generally do not change much over a single day. However, accounting for time-of-day effects reduces the amount of unexplained variation in the data, thus improving the precision of the analysis.

Seasonal differences in weather, amount of daylight, and weekend recreational travel can affect driving speeds, and inasmuch as they are related to the demand for gasoline, those differences can also affect the price of gasoline. CBO's analysis accounts for seasonal effects.

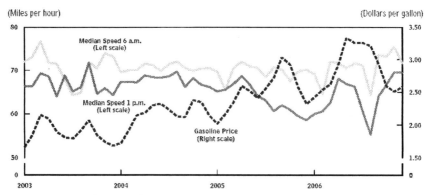

Sources: Congressional Budget Office based on data from the Freeway Performance
    Measurement Project, https://pems.eecs.berkeley.edu.
Note: Speeds were recorded at 6 a.m. and 1 p.m. each Saturday and Sunday from 2003
    to 2006 by sensors located on southbound Interstate 405 at Newland Street,
    Westminster, California. Prices are nominal average California retail gasoline
    prices for all grades and formulations.
Figure A-3. Median Weekend Speeds on I-405, Orange County, California, and
Gasoline Prices.

Figure A-3 shows the overall structure of the data. It reports median weekend speeds from 2003 to 2006 (for the sake of clarity it shows only one location and two periods: 6 a.m. to 7 a.m. and 1 p.m. to 2 p.m.) and the statewide monthly average gasoline price for all grades and formulations.[9] At the I-405 location, median speeds are often 4 mph to 5 mph slower in the afternoon than they are in the early morning. The difference could result from higher traffic volume in the middle of the day. It also could be that traffic enforcement is more rigorous at that time of day.

Median speeds at the I-405 location appear to have fallen slightly from 2004 to 2006, as gasoline prices were rising. CBO's analysis estimates the influence of higher gas prices on vehicle speeds, controlling for other possible factors that also could have caused a change in median (and other percentile) vehicle speeds. Those factors are described in Appendix B.

The figure shows that median speeds at the I-405 location dropped sharply in mid-2003 and again in mid-2006. Such a pattern (also found at different times at the other two locations) can be caused by chronic congestion (lasting a month or more), as from road construction. That data pattern also could have been caused by an offline vehicle detector station (in which case imputed data are substituted). In all such cases, CBO flagged the data, thus neutralizing their effect on the analysis. For technical reasons, CBO did not exclude those observations altogether, because doing so would have removed all of the contemporaneous data from the other locations.

End Notes

[1] The data are provided by the Freeway Performance Measurement Project, a joint effort of the University of California at Berkeley, the California Department of Transportation, California Partners for Advanced Transit and Highways, and Berkeley Transportation Systems. See *Freeway Performance Measurement System,* https:// pems.eecs.berkeley.edu.

[2] In some cases, data from a location were of insufficient quality, so a nearby location was chosen instead. Data quality suffers when electronic detector stations go offline. In those cases, the Freeway Performance Measurement Project imputes values from nearby detectors. For lengthy outages, however, the imputed data are not usable for CBO's purposes because their day-to-day variance is too low (often zero).

[3] Technically, the analysis fits a second-degree trend line to the data, so that the trend can be a straight line or have the shape of an upward or downward "U." Restricting the trend to be a straight line (constraining it from curving) resulted in very similar conclusions.

[4] See Congressional Budget Office, *China's Growing Demand for Oil and Its Impact on U.S. Petroleum Markets* (April 2006).

[5] The results are also consistent with the possibility that drivers of less-fuel-efficient vehicles tend to drive more slowly and are more responsive to increases in gasoline prices. However, such a possibility also would imply that those drivers have lower values of time than do owners of more-fuel-efficient vehicles.

[6] Most months have eight weekend days, so a one-time congestion event lasting 45 minutes would affect observed speeds only up to the 10th percentile (45 minutes out of 8 hours of traffic observed), and only for that time of day.

[7] For the purposes of its analysis, CBO defined congestion as 5th percentile speeds below 55 miles per hour, median speeds of 60 mph or slower, and 95th percentile speeds slower than

65 mph. Between 1 percent and 3 percent of observed speeds are below those thresholds. Of the three locations surveyed, I-405 in Orange County experienced the greatest frequency of temporary slowdowns: Its slowest 5th percentile speed (for all times of day) was below 40 mph in 32 of 48 months, and it was faster than 55 mph only twice. On I-680 in San Ramon there were 7 months below 40 mph, 27 months above 55 mph, and 12 months above 60 mph. In contrast, I-8 in San Diego had only 1 month below 40 mph and only 5 months below 50 mph; it had 41 months above 55 mph and 31 months with 5th percentile speeds above 60 mph.

[8] Fixed effects also would control for differences in the stringency with which speed limits are enforced, if the agency charged with that enforcement, the California Highway Patrol, consistently allocates its enforcement resources on the basis of historic differences in accident rates or other criteria.

[9] The prices are averages of nominal posted prices from a survey of gasoline stations around California. CBO's analysis adjusts prices for inflation. Prices vary slightly by metropolitan area in this study, but price movements are highly correlated.

In: Gasoline Prices and their Effects on Behavior   ISBN: 978-1-60741-351-6
Editor: Hermann Schreiber   © 2010 Nova Science Publishers, Inc.

Chapter 4

APPENDIX B. ANALYTICAL APPROACH AND ECONOMETRIC RESULTS

Congressional Budget Office

For this analysis, the Congressional Budget Office (CBO) modeled preferred driving speeds at a given location as a function of the price of gasoline, time of day, month (time of year), average value of time, fixed physical characteristics of the freeway at that location (including grade, curvature, speed limit, and distance to nearest on- and off-ramps), and the overall demand for weekend travel in that month at that location. The time-of-day and time-of-year factors control for the effects of variation in the amount of daylight and in average weather conditions, as well as possible variations in the types of trips motorists make at different times of day or season. The average wage rate is a proxy for motorists' value of time.[1]

The travel demand term captures changes over time in average traffic density, or the median number of vehicles per day on weekends at each location, per month. That factor controls for the effect that overall traffic density, or proximity to other vehicles, might have on motorists' preferred speeds even under relatively free-flowing weekend driving conditions. Thus, the model estimates the effect of gasoline prices on vehicle speeds independently of the effects of increased travel demand and other factors. The model also includes dummy variables for high and low outliers associated with imputed data and for speeds that are slow enough to indicate possible congestion. Finally, as a measure of data quality, the model includes the percentage of time the vehicle detection equipment was online that month, in case the measurements the equipment provides are correlated with the fraction of time that the equipment is functioning properly.

The data are organized as a panel, with each location–hour constituting a cross section. The main analysis examines the median (or 5th or 95th percentile) speeds for 11 one-hour periods of the day, observed over every Saturday and Sunday each month, at each of three locations. Thus the panel comprises 33 cross-sectional observations, with a time-step of 1 month and 48 months of observations. The percentile speed statistic for one cross section (summarizing observed speeds within a given hour of the day at a given location) might not be independent of that for another cross section (a different hour at the same location, or the same or a different hour at another location). CBO fit the data to an ordinary least-squares (OLS) model of the following form:

$$y_{it} = \sum_{k=1}^{K} X_{itk}\beta_k + u_{it}$$

$$i = 1, \ldots, N; t = 1, \ldots, T \tag{1}$$

but computed panel-corrected standard errors (PCSE) $\hat{u}_{it}$ that allow for such a structure among the errors.[2] In Equation (1), the y_{it} term is the Qth percentile (for example, the median) vehicle speed on the weekend at location–hour i in month t. N is the number of location–hour cross sections (here, 33), T is the number of months observed (48), K is the number of exogenous regressors X in the model, and β is a vector of parameters to be estimated. The statistical significance of the fitted parameters β_k depends on the PCSE term $\hat{u}_{it}$, which contains the square roots of the diagonal terms in the following expression:

$$(X'X)^{-1} X' \hat{\Omega} X (X'X)^{-1} \tag{2}$$

In Equation (2), $\hat{\Omega}$ is an $NT \times NT$ block-diagonal matrix formed from the panel structure of N cross sections and T time periods, with each block comprising an $N \times N$ matrix $\hat{\Sigma}_{ij}$ of terms of the form $e_{it}e_{jt}$, each term the product of the OLS residuals for cross sections i and j at time t:

$$\hat{\Sigma}_{ij} = \frac{\sum_{t=1}^{T} e_{it}e_{jt}}{T} \tag{3}$$

The results indicate that the model fits the data reasonably well, with R^2 values in excess of 0.5. Sample statistics are reported in Table B-1 on page 34; results are reported in Table B-2 on page 35.[3]

TOTAL TRIPS

The vehicle count data have a substantially different structure from the data on vehicle speeds, which are expressed as a distribution summarizing the speeds that were observed each month and the frequency of occurrence for each speed. In contrast, vehicle counts are observed directly and pertain to travel on a single day.

The data consist of total daily vehicle counts at each of a dozen locations around California on every Wednesday, Saturday, and Sunday from April 2003 through December 2006.[4] Because of differences in capacity, local population density, and patterns of travel demand, vehicle counts vary substantially more from one location to the next than do vehicle speeds. To pool the data into a panel, CBO expressed the vehicle counts as a fraction of the baseline mean vehicle count at each location, using nonholiday Wednesdays in January 2003 (several months before the period covered in the analysis) as the baseline.

With vehicle counts, there is less likelihood of contemporaneous correlation between cross sections than there is with the speed data, because no two cross-sectional (location–day) counts are collected on the same day at the same location. Also, as the analysis shows, counts at different locations respond slightly differently to changes in gasoline prices, depending partly on the ease of access to public transportation at each location.

Thus, CBO fit a one-way, fixed-effects model to the data, with a separate fixed effect for each location–day. The fixed effects control not only for day-of-week differences in volume of traffic at each location relative to the baseline but also for differences among locations in population density, proximity to residential or employment locations, and existence of alternative routes or modes of travel. As an alternative specification, a two-way, fixed-effects model would fit separate effects also for each week (1 83 weeks total). However, CBO takes the more parsimonious approach described below.

Table B-1. Sample Means and Vehicle Speeds, January 2003 to December 2006

	Mean	Standard Deviation	Minimum	Maximum
	Hour-Specific Monthly Percentiles (Analyzed Hours Only)			
5th Percentile Speed[a]	62.8	8.3	8.7	78.1
Median Speed[a]	67.8	4.1	40.1	78.8
95th Percentile Speed[a]	70.8	3.3	53.9	79.1
Median Traffic Density[b]	4.2	1.72	0.47	7.86
95th Percentile Traffic Density[b]	5.06	1.75	0.74	8.99
	Other Continuous Variables			
Real Retail Gasoline Price (Dollars per gallon)[c]	2.38	0.40	1.75	3.28
Real Wages (Dollars per hour)[d]	16.46	0.26	15.78	16.85
Daily Percent Uptime, Detector	86.1	18.6	12.5	100
	Indicator Variables			
Month Effects	1/12	0.3	0	1
Early Morning (6–8 a.m., by route)	0.06	0.24	0	1
Prime I (9 a.m.–1 p.m., by route)	0.12	0.33	0	1
Prime II (2–6 p.m., by route)	0.06	0.24	0	1
Evening (7–9 p.m., by route)	0.06	0.24	0	1
Night (10 p.m.–midnight., by route)	0.03	0.17	0	1
	Congestion and Data Anomaly Indicators			
5th Percentile Speed <55 mph	0.12	0.32	0	1
Median speed <60 mph	0.02	0.14	0	1
95th Percentile Speed <65 mph	0.02	0.14	0	1
Low-Speed Outliers[e]	0.07	0.27	0	1
High-Speed Outliers[e]	0.06	0.23	0	1

Source: Congressional Budget Office based on data from the Freeway Performance Measurement Project, https://pems.eecs.berkeley.edu.

Note: Hours analyzed are 6, 8, 9, and 11 a.m.; noon; and 1, 4, 5, 7, 8, and 10 p.m. Analysis results are not dependent on that specific set of hours.

a. Miles per hour.

b. Thousands of vehicles per hour.

c. Average monthly retail price for all grades and formulations, adjusted for inflation (base period January 2006). Data from the Department of Energy, Energy Information Administration.

d. Adjusted for inflation (base period January 2006). Data from the Department of Commerce, Bureau of Labor Statistics.

e. Denotes sustained periods of low- or high-speed anomalies in the data (congestion indicators capture brief, temporary slowdowns only).

Table B-2. Vehicle Speeds and Gasoline Prices, Primary Econometric Results

(Miles per hour)	5th Percentile		Median		95th Percentile	
	Speed	Std. Error	Speed	Std. Error	Speed	Std. Error
Intercept	85.2 **	17.4	55.3 **	16.3	61.6 **	14.0
Real Retail Gasoline Price[a]	-0.024 **	0.005	-0.015 **	0.004	-0.001	0.004
Traffic Density[b]	-0.33 *	0.15	-0.49 **	0.10	-0.14	0.10
Real Wages	-1.04	1.06	0.91	1.00	0.54	0.86
(Time-of-Day X Route) Effects						
Early Morning (6–8 a.m.)						
I-680, San Ramon	1.20	0.92	0.94	0.60	2.44 **	0.46
I-405, Westminster	3.61 **	0.66	2.39 **	0.56	3.77 **	0.60
I-8, San Diego	3.56 **	0.81	1.21 *	0.61	1.64 **	0.64
Prime I (9 a.m.–1 p.m.)						
I-680, San Ramon	-0.14	0.63	-0.46	0.33	1.08 *	0.45
I-405, Westminster	0.23	0.83	0.90	0.65	1.54 *	0.64
I-8, San Diego	2.79 **	0.82	1.65 **	0.59	1.27 **	0.59
Prime II (2–6 p.m.)						
I-680, San Ramon	(Omitted Factor)					
I-405, Westminster	-0.85	1.14	0.13	0.71	0.95	0.64
I-8, San Diego	3.34 **	0.82	1.85 **	0.57	1.21 *	0.59
Evening (7–9 p.m.)						
I-680, San Ramon	0.35	0.59	0.45	0.24	0.02	0.30
I-405, Westminster	2.32 **	0.81	1.30 *	0.65	1.45 *	0.62

Table B-2. (Continued)

(Miles per hour)	5th Percentile		Median		95th Percentile	
	Speed	Std. Error	Speed	Std. Error	Speed	Std. Error
I-8, San Diego	2.94 **	0.81	0.99	0.57	0.48	0.64
			Night (10 p.m.–Midnight)			
I-680, San Ramon	0.75	0.77	-0.15	0.47	0.19	0.43
I-405, Westminster	1.81 *	0.86	1.47 *	0.66	2.48 **	0.63
I-8, San Diego	1.78	0.94	-0.58	0.59	-0.03	0.66
			Significance			
Month Effects	Jointly significant		Jointly significant		Not significant	
Congestion, Outlier Flags	**		**		**	
Detector Percent Online	0.02 *	0.01	0.02 *	0.01	0.003	0.009
R-squared	0.718		0.613		0.523	

Source: Congressional Budget Office based on data from the Freeway Performance Measurement Project, https://pems.eecs.berkeley.edu. Notes: Std. = standard; ** = significant at 1 percent; * = significant at 5 percent; I = Interstate. Hours analyzed are 6, 8, 9, and 11 a.m.; noon; and 1, 4, 5, 7, 8, and 10 p.m. Results are very similar for an analysis of entirely different hours, for the exclusion of prime hours, or both. Panel structure is 33 cross-sections (3 locations × 11 hours) for 48 months.

a. Average monthly price for all grades and formulations.

b. Thousands of vehicles per hour, either median (middle column) or 95th percentile densities (outside columns) for a given time of day on the weekend, in the same month, at a given location. Panel structure is 33 cross-sections (3 locations × 11 hours) for 48 months.

Table B-3. Sample Means for Total Daily Vehicles, April 2003 to December 2006

	Mean	Standard Deviation	Minimum	Maximum
Total Vehicles (Relative to baseline average, 1:1 = 100)	88.6	13.2	28.2	184.2
Real Average Weekly Retail Gasoline Price (Relative to baseline period; all grades, all formulations; 1:1 = 100)	111.2	18.6	79.4	152.5
Real Average Weekly Retail Gasoline Price (All grades, all formulations, dollars per gallon)	2.42	0.40	1.73	3.32
Daily Percent Uptime, Detector Station	81.5	34.8	0	100
Indicator Variables				
Detector Offline All Day	0.13	0.33	0	1
Day 1 of 3-Day Holiday[a]	0.05	0.22	0	1
Day 2 of 3-Day Holiday[b]	0.05	0.22	0	1
Day 3 of 3-Day Holiday[c]	0.02	0.12	0	1
Veterans Day Weekend[d]	0.02	0.15	0	1
Summer Weekend[e]	0.22	0.41	0	1

Source: Congressional Budget Office based on data from the Freeway Performance Measurement Project, https://pems.eecs.berkeley.edu.

Note: n = 6,558

a. Includes Wednesdays on the eve of Thanksgiving, Christmas, and New Year's Day. (There were no Wednesday holidays from April 2003 to December 2006.)

b. Includes Saturday of Thanksgiving week.

c. Includes Sunday of Thanksgiving week.

d. Veterans Day is a fixed-date holiday that was observed on a Friday in 2005 and 2006.

e. May 23 to September 6, the dates of the earliest Memorial Day Saturday and latest Labor Day Sunday from 2003 to 2006. Weekends constitute two-thirds of the data; one-third of the data fall between May 23 and September 6 because the data that CBO analyzed date from April 2003.

Table B-4. Total Trips and Gasoline Prices, Primary Econometric Results

	Dependent Variable				
	Total Daily Vehicles[a]	Standard Error	Net Effect	F Test	(p > F)
Intercept	94.9 **	1.08			
Real Relative Price of Gasoline[b]	-0.0002	0.011		0.00	0.99
Price × Weekend	0.0003	0.009	0.0001	0.00	0.99
Price × Rail	-0.034 **	0.013	-0.034	12.42 **	0.004
Price × Weekend × Rail	0.044 **	0.012	0.01	1.33	0.25
Summer Weekends	0.475	0.22			
Day 1, Holiday Period	-2.65 **	0.26			
Day 2, Holiday Period	-3.16 **	0.27			
Day 3, holiday period	-3.02 **	0.48			
Veterans Day Weekend	3.19 **	0.44	0.03 (Sat), 0.17 (Sun)		
Percent Uptime	0.024 **	0.004			
	Significance				
Location Trends	Jointly significant			5.95 **	0.0001
Location Squared Trends	Jointly significant			14.78 **	0.0001
Month Effects	Jointly significant			27.49 **	0.0001
Cross-Section Effects	All significant at 1 percent				

Source: Congressional Budget Office based on data from the Freeway Performance Measurement Project, https://pems.eecs.berkeley.edu.

Notes: $p > F$ = statistical significance; **= significant at 1 percent; Sat = Saturday; Sun = Sunday.

Exclusion of squared-trend terms yields similar results. Panel structure is 36 cross sections (12 locations x 3 days) for 183 weeks.

a. Relative to baseline (1:1 = 100).

b. Average weekly retail price, all grades and formulations (relative to 2003 baseline price).

The analysis models the daily relative vehicle count at each location as a function of the price of gasoline, with separate price effects estimated for weekdays and weekends and for locations where rail transit either is or is not accessible. The model also allows for quadratic location- specific trends in vehicle totals, and it includes fixed effects for the month and indicators for holiday travel (estimated separately as effects for the first, middle, or final day of multiple-day holiday travel periods, as appropriate); summer weekends (which can feature above-average travel); nonholiday outliers; and, to control for differences in data quality, a continuous measure of the percentage of time each vehicle detector station was not operating and an indicator for zero percent observed (meaning that the observation in question was imputed entirely).

Up to the error term, the model for daily total vehicles has same the form as that used for Equation (1). Here, the error term has the following form:

$$u_{it} = v_i + \varepsilon_{it}$$

(4)

where, as before, the ε_{it} are mean-zero, independent, identically distributed errors (although in this model, the cross-term covariances are assumed to be zero), and v_i is the fixed-effect term for each location–day cross section i.

The model fits the data well, with R^2 terms of nearly 0.9. A standard statistical F test strongly rejects the hypothesis of no route–day fixed effects, and a Hausman test strongly rejects an alternative specification with random effects as opposed to fixed effects.[5] Sample statistics are reported in Table B-3 on page 36; results are reported in Table B-4 on page 37.

End Notes

[1] Using the average gross hourly wage in the analysis yields the same outcome as would using the hourly wage, net of taxes (because the analysis is not done at the level of the individual motorist). Both are statewide values that vary only over time, at approximately the same rate: The effect of any changes in marginal tax rates on the average net hourly wage would be very small.

[2] See Nathaniel Beck and Jonathan N. Katz, "What to Do (and Not to Do) with Time-Series Cross-Section Data," *American Political Science Review*, vol. 89 (September 1995), pp. 634–647.

[3] CBO also analyzed the data using the Parks method, a related but older and now less common technique that produces unbiased parameter estimates but that can underestimate the standard errors (thus overestimating the precision of the estimates). See Richard Parks, "Efficient Estimation of a System of Regression Equations When Disturbances Are Both Serially and Contemporaneously Correlated," *Journal of the American Statistical Association*, vol. 62 (1967), pp. 500–509. In CBO's analysis, the Parks method yielded qualitatively similar results.

[4] Earlier data can be analyzed for most routes, but at the cost of excluding, for computational reasons, routes lacking any earlier data. However, results are generally unchanged if such routes are excluded from the analysis.

[5] See J.A. Hausman, "Specification Tests in Econometrics," *Econometrica,* vol. 46, no. 6 (1978), pp. 1251–1271.

In: Gasoline Prices and their Effects on Behavior   ISBN: 978-1-60741-351-6
Editor: Hermann Schreiber   © 2010 Nova Science Publishers, Inc.

Chapter 5

REFERENCES

Congressional Budget Office

Armen Alchian & William Allen (1964). *Exchange and Production: Competition, Coordination, and Control* (Belmont, Calif.: Wadsworth, 1983; originally published as *University Economics: Elements of Inquiry*).

American Petroleum Institute, "Gasoline Taxes, October (2006)," www.api.org/policy/tax/stateexcise/uploadoctober_2006_gasoline_and_di esel_summary _pages.pdf.

Bureau of Labor Statistics, May (2006). State Occupational Employment and Wage Estimates, California, www.bls.gov/oes/current/oes_ca.htm.

Charles A. Lave (1985). "Speeding, Coordination, and the 55-MPH Limit," *American Economic Review, vol. 75*, no. 5, pp. 1159–1 164.

California Franchise Tax Board (2006). California Tax Table, www.ftb.ca.gov/forms/06_forms/ 06_540tt.pdf.

Congressional Budget Office(2002). *Reducing Gasoline Consumption: Three Policy Options* (November).

Congressional Budget Office (2003). *The Economic Costs of Fuel Economy Standards Versus a Gasoline Tax* (December).

Congressional Budget Office, *Budget Options* (February 2005), Option 32, p. 308.

Congressional Budget Office (2005). *Effective Marginal Tax Rates on Labor Income* (November).

Congressional Budget Office (2006). *China's Growing Demand for Oil and Its Impact on U. S. Petroleum Markets* (April).

Congressional Budget Office (2006). *The Economic Effects of Recent Increases in Energy Prices* (July).

Carol A. Dahl (1979). "Consumer Adjustment to a Gasoline Tax," *Review of Economics and Statistics, vol. 61,* no. 3, pp. 427–432.

Carmen DeNavas-Walt, Bernadette D. Proctor & Cheryl Hill Lee (2006). *Income, Poverty, and Health Insurance Coverage in the United States: 2005,* Current Population Reports P60-231 (Bureau of the Census, August), p. 6, Table 1, "Income and Earnings Summary Measures by Selected Characteristics: 2004 and 2005," www.census.gov/prod/2006pubs/ p60-231 .pdf.

C.T. Jones (1993). "Another Look at U.S. Passenger Vehicle Use and the 'Rebound' Effect from Improved Fuel Efficiency," *Energy Journal, vol. 14,* no. 4, pp. 99–110.

David Brownstone & others (2003). "Drivers' Willingness-toPay to Reduce Travel Time: Evidence from the San Diego I-15 Congestion Pricing Project," Transportation Research, Part A: *Policy and Practice, vol. 37,* pp. 372–387.

Department of Energy, Energy Information Administration, *U.S. Retail Gasoline Prices,* www.eia.doe.gov/ oil_gas/petroleum/data _publications/wrgp/ mogas_home_page.html.

Department of Energy (2007). Energy Information Administration, p. 132, Table 9.4, Motor Gasoline Retail Prices, U.S. City Average, *Monthly Energy Review* (October), www.eia.doe.gov/emeu/mer/pdf/pages/sec9_6.pdf.

David Grabowski & Michael Morrisey (2004). "Gasoline Prices and Motor Vehicle Fatalities," *Journal of Policy Analysis and Management, vol. 23,* no. 3, pp. 575–593.

David Grabowski & Michael Morrisey (2006). "Do Higher Gasoline Taxes Save Lives?" *Economics Letters, vol. 90,* pp. 5 1–55.

Daniel Graham & Stephen Glaister (2002). "The Demand for Automobile Fuel: A Survey of Elasticities," *Journal of Transport Economics and Policy, vol. 36,* pp. 1–26.

David L. Greene, James Kahn & Gibson, R. (1999). "Fuel Economy Rebound Effect for U.S. Household Vehicles," *Energy Journal, vol. 20,* no. 3, pp. 1–31.

Environmental Protection Agency, *Fuel Economy,* www epa.gov/ fuel economy.

Environmental Protection Agency (1999). *Gasoline Fuels, Reformulated Gasoline Emission Facts,* EPA420-F-99-040 (November), www.epa.gov/otaq/f99040.htm.

Environmental Protection Agency, Office of Transportation and Air Quality, Compliance and Innovative Strategies Division and Transportation Compliance Division, *Light-Duty Automotive Technology and Fuel Economy Trends: 1975 Through 2007,* EPA420-R-07-008 (September 2007), p. A-9, www.epa.gov/otaq/cert/mpg/fetrends/ 420r07008a.pdf.

Federal Trade Commission, Gasoline Price Changes (2005). *The Dynamic of Supply, Demand, and Competition,* www.ftc.gov/reports/gasprices05/ 050705gaspricesrpt.pdf.

Federal Trade Commission (2006). *Investigation of Gasoline Price Manipulation and Post-Katrina Gasoline Price Increases,* www.ftc.gov/reports/060518PublicGasolinePricesInvestigationReport Final.pdf.

George G. Daly & Thomas H. Mayor (1983). "Reason and Rationality During Energy Crises," *Journal of Political Economy, vol. 19,* no. 1, pp. 168–181.

Haughton, J. & Sarker, S. (1996). "Gasoline Tax as a Corrective Tax: Estimates for the United States. 1970–1991," *Energy Journal, vol. 17,* no. 2, pp. 103–126.

Hausman, J. A. (1978). "Specification Tests in Econometrics," *Econometrica, vol. 46,* no. 6, pp. 1251–1271.

Ian W.H. Parry and Kenneth A. Small (2005). "Does Britain or the United States Have the Right Gasoline Tax?" *American Economic Review, vol. 95,* no. 4, pp. 1276–1289.

John Greenlees (1980). "Gasoline Prices and Purchases of New Automobiles," *Southern Economic Journal, vol. 47,* no. 1, pp. 167–178.

Jonathan E. Hughes, Christopher R. Knittel, & Daniel Sperling (2006). *Evidence of a Shift in the Short-Run Price Elasticity of Gasoline Demand,* Research Report UCD-ITS-RR-06- 16 (University of California, Davis: Institute of Transportation Studies,).

James Kahn (1986). "Gasoline Prices and the Used Automobile Market: A Rational Expectations Asset Price Approach," Quarterly *Journal of Economics, vol. 101,* no. 2, pp. 323–340.

Joshua Linn and Thomas Klier (2007). "Gasoline Prices and the Demand for New Vehicles: Evidence from Monthly Sales Data" (working paper, March), http://tigger.uic.edu/~jlinn/vehicles

Kenneth A. Small, (1992). *Urban Transportation Economics, vol. 51 of Fundamentals of Pure and Applied Economics* (Newark, N.J.: Harwood Academic Publishers), p. 44.

Kenneth A. Small & Kurt Van Dender (2007). "Fuel Efficiency and Motor Vehicle Travel: The Declining Rebound Effect," *Energy Journal, vol. 28,* no. 1, pp. 25–51; and corrections posted at www.socsci.uci.edu/ ~ksmall/Rebound_Paper _Correction.pdf.

Kenneth A. Small, Clifford Winston & Jia Yan (2005). "Uncovering the Distribution of Motorists' Preferences for Travel Time and Reliability," *Econometrica, vol. 73*, no. 4, pp. 1367–1382.

Kevin Washbrook, Wolfgang Haider & Mark Jaccard (2006). "Estimating Commuter Mode Choice: A Discrete Choice Analysis of the Impact of Road Pricing and Parking Charges," *Transportation, vol. 33,* no. 6, pp. 621–639.

Michael Morris, *"Short-Run Motor Gasoline Demand Model"* (presentation at the Energy Outlook, Modeling and Data Conference, Department of Energy, Energy Information Administration, Washington, D.C., March 28, 2007), www.eia.doe.gov/oiaf/aeo/ conf/pdf/morris.pdf.

Marilouise Burgess, *Contrasting Rural & Urban Fatal Crashes (1994–2003).* NHTSA Technical Report DOT HS 809 896 (Department of Transportation, National Highway Traffic Safety Administration, December 2005, Table 3, p.19, www-nrd.nhtsa.dot.gov/Pubs/809896.PDF).

Matthew E. Kahn (2000). "The Environmental Impact of Sub- urbanization," *Journal of Policy Analysis and Management, vol. 19*, no. 4, pp. 569–586.

Nathaniel Beck & Jonathan N. Katz (1995). "What to Do (and Not to Do) with Time-Series Cross-Section Data," *American Political Science Review, vol. 89* (September), pp. 634–647.

Nils Bruzelius, *The Value of Travel Time: Theory and Measurement* (London: Croom Helm, 1979).

National Highway Traffic Safety Administration, *"CAFE Overview, Frequently Asked Questions,"* www.nhtsa.dot.gov/cars/rules/cafe/overview.htm.

National Research Council, *Effectiveness and Impact of Corporate Average Fuel Economy (CAFE) Standards* (Washington, D.C.: National Academy Press, 2002), available from www.nap.edu/catalog.php?record _id=10172.

Orley Ashenfelter & Michael Greenstone (2004). "Using Mandated Speed Limits to Measure the Value of a Statistical Life," *Journal of Political Economy, vol. 112*, no. 1, pp. S226–S267.

Robert T. Deacon & Jon Sonstelie (1985). "Rationing by Waiting and the Value of Time: Results from a Natural Experiment," *Journal of Political Economy, vol. 93*, no. 1, pp. 627–647.

Robert M. Heavenrich, *Light-Duty Automotive Technology & Fuel Economy Trends (2006). 1975 Through 2006,* EPA420-R-06-0 11 (Environmental Protection Agency, Office of Transportation and Air Quality, Advanced Technology Division, July), p. A-10, *www.epa.gov/otaq/cert/ mpg/fetrends*/420r0601 1.pdf.

Robert Lawson & Lauren Raymer, "Testing the Alchian–Allen Theorem: A Study of Consumer Behavior in the Gasoline Market," *Economics Bulletin, vol. 4,* issue 35 (2006), pp. 1–6, http:// economicsbulletin.vanderbilt.edu/2006/volume4/ EB-06D0002 1A.pdf.

Richard Parks (1967). "Efficient Estimation of a System of Regression Equations When Disturbances Are Both Serially and Contemporaneously Correlated," *Journal of the American Statistical Association, vol. 62*, pp. 500–509.

Richard Voith (1991). "The Long-Run Elasticity of Commuter Rail Demand," *Journal of Urban Economics, vol. 30*, pp. 360–372.

Richard Voith (1997). "Fares, Service Levels, and Demographics: What Determines Commuter Rail Ridership in the Long Run?" *Journal of Urban Economics, vol. 41*, pp. 176–197.

Stacy C. Davis (2001). *Transportation Energy Data Book: Edition 21-2001,* ORNL-6966 (prepared by Oak Ridge National Laboratory for the Department of Energy Office of Transportation Technologies, October), Tables 7.21 and 7.22, www.ornl.gov/ ~webworks/cppr/y200 1/rpt/ 111 858.pdf.

Steven Polzin & Xuehao Chu (2005). *Public Transit in America: Results from the 2001 National Household Travel Survey,* BC137-48 (Tampa: National Center for Transit Research, University of South Florida, September), www.nctr.usf.edu/pdf/527-09.pdf.

Sarah West (2007). "The Effect of Gasoline Prices on the Demand for Sport Utility Vehicles" (prepared for a session on "Demand Estimation in Environmental Economics," Midwest Economics Association Meetings, March), www.macalester.edu/ ~wests/SarahWestMEA2007.pdf.

Theodore E. Keeler (1994). "Highway Safety, Economic Behavior, and Driving Environment," *American Economic Review, vol. 84,* no. 3, pp. 684–693.

Todd M. Nesbit (2005). *Excise Taxation and Product Quality: The Gasoline Market,* Working Paper 05-11 (Morgantown: West Virginia

University, Department of Economics), www.be.wvu.edu/div/econ//work/ pdf_files/05-1 1 .pdf.

University of California at Berkeley, California Department of Transportation, California Partners for Advanced Transit and Highways, and Berkeley Transportation Systems, "*Freeway Performance Measurement Project,*" https://pems.eecs .berkeley.edu.

West, B. H. & others (1999). *Development and Validation of Light-Duty Modal Emissions and Fuel Consumption Values for Traffic Models,* FHWA-RD-99-068 (Federal Highway Administration,).

Walter McManus (2007). "The Link Between Gasoline Prices and Vehicle Sales: Economic Theory Trumps Conventional Detroit Wisdom," *Business Economics,* (January), pp. 53–60.

Yoram Barzel (1976). "An Alternative Approach to Analysis and Taxation," *Journal of Political Economy, vol. 84,* no. 6, pp. 1177–1 197.

Young-Jun Kweon & Kara Kockelman (2006). "Driver Attitudes and Choices: Speed Limits, Seat Belt Use, and Drinking-and-Driving," *Journal of Transportation Research Forum, vol. 45,* no. 3, pp. 39–56.

INDEX